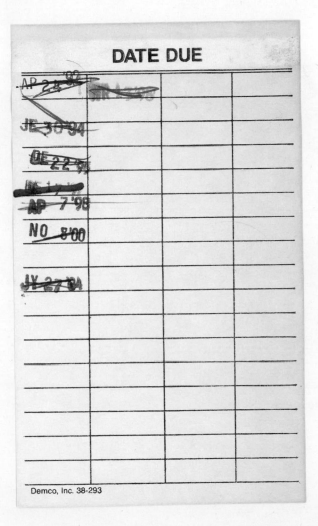

U.S. HANDS OFF THE MIDEAST!

Cuba speaks out at the United Nations

U.S. HANDS OFF THE MIDEAST!

Cuba speaks out at the United Nations

FIDEL CASTRO
RICARDO ALARCON

PATHFINDER

New York   London   Montréal   Sydney

Edited by Mary-Alice Waters

ISBN 0-87348-629-3 paper; ISBN 0-87348-630-7 cloth
Library of Congress Catalog Card Number 90-63931
Manufactured in the United States of America

First edition, October 1990
Second edition, November 1990

Security Council resolutions are from the United Nations record. The texts of Ricardo Alarcón's remarks are taken from transcriptions of the simultaneous translation provided by the United Nations. All other material is from *Granma,* the daily newspaper of the Communist Party of Cuba. Translations have been checked against the Spanish and edited by Pathfinder.

This book is also available in Spanish.

Design by Toni Gorton

PATHFINDER
410 West Street, New York, NY 10014, U.S.A.

Pathfinder distributors around the world:
Australia (and Asia and the Pacific):
 Pathfinder, 19 Terry St., Surry Hills, Sydney, NSW 2010
Britain (and Europe, Africa, and the Middle East):
 Pathfinder, 47 The Cut, London, SE1 8LL
Canada:
 Pathfinder, 6566, boul. St-Laurent, Montréal, Québec, H2S 3C6
Iceland:
 Pathfinder, Klapparstíg 26, 2d floor, 121 Reykjavík
New Zealand:
 Pathfinder, 157a Symonds Street, Auckland
Sweden:
 Pathfinder, Vikingagatan 10, S-113 42, Stockholm
United States (and Caribbean and Latin America):
 Pathfinder, 410 West Street, New York, NY 10014

Cover photo: U.S. M-1 tanks on patrol between Dhahran and Riyadh, Saudi Arabia, September 1990. (Patrick Durand/Sygma)

CONTENTS

Fidel Castro

Born in 1926, Fidel Castro entered politics while attending the University of Havana in the mid-1940s.

After Fulgencio Batista's coup d'état in 1952, Castro organized a revolutionary movement to oust the U.S.-backed dictatorship. On July 26, 1953, he led an attack on the Moncada army garrison in Santiago de Cuba. While unsuccessful in realizing its immediate aims, this attack initiated a revolutionary campaign that culminated in the armed uprising that forced Batista to flee Cuba on January 1, 1959.

In February 1959 Castro became prime minister, a post he held until December 1976, when he became president of the Council of State and the Council of Ministers. He has been commander in chief of Cuba's armed forces since 1959 and is first secretary of the Central Committee of the Communist Party of Cuba.

Ricardo Alarcón

Born in 1937, Ricardo Alarcón was a leader of the July 26 Movement at the University of Havana during the struggle against Batista. After the revolution's victory, he served as president of the Federation of University Students. From 1966 to 1978 he was Cuba's permanent representative to the United Nations. He was named deputy foreign minister in 1978, and became first deputy foreign minister in 1989. Since 1980 he has been an alternate member of the Central Committee of the Communist Party of Cuba.

In the 1980s Alarcón was Cuba's chief negotiator with the U.S. government, leading Cuba's efforts to reach immigration agreements with Washington in 1984 and 1987. He participated in the 1988 talks involving Cuba, Angola, South Africa, and the United States, which led to the withdrawal of South African troops from Angola and the independence of Namibia.

Alarcón was renamed Cuba's permanent representative to the United Nations at the end of 1989, following Cuba's election to a two-year term on the Security Council.

THE GULF REGION

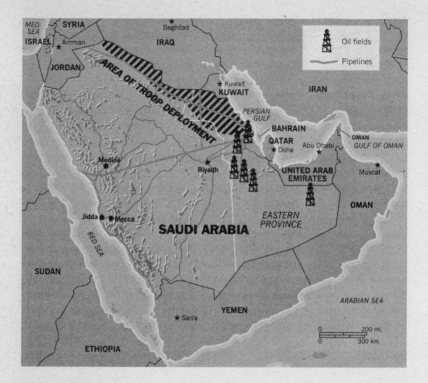

Oil fields
Pipelines

MED.
SEA
SYRIA
ISRAEL
Amman
JORDAN
Baghdad
IRAQ
Kuwait
KUWAIT
IRAN
AREA OF TROOP DEPLOYMENT
PERSIAN
GULF
BAHRAIN
QATAR
Doha
Abu Dhabi
OMAN
GULF OF OMAN
Medina
Riyadh
UNITED ARAB
EMIRATES
Muscat
Jidda
Mecca
SAUDI ARABIA
EASTERN
PROVINCE
OMAN
SUDAN
RED SEA
YEMEN
San'a
ARABIAN SEA
0   200 mi.
0   300 km.
ETHIOPIA

INTRODUCTION

● Since August 2, 1990, the U.S. government has been preparing systematically and on a massive scale for a war against Iraq. The pace of these preparations is accelerating.

● Washington is using the unanimous votes of the five permanent members of the United Nations Security Council to give cover to the U.S. buildup and unilateral acts of aggression, while obstructing initiatives aimed at seeking a peaceful solution to the crisis.

● The U.S. rulers' escalating war moves since the invasion of Kuwait by the Iraqi government are not motivated by support for national sovereignty and territorial integrity. The invasion of Kuwait has been seized upon by the U.S. government as an unforeseen opportunity to advance its imperialist interests.

● Working people the world over are already paying dearly for the U.S.-organized war preparations. The cost in lives and economic well-being will be incalculable if efforts to avoid a war continue to be blocked by Washington.

● All those concerned about the accelerating buildup of this U.S.-organized death machine have a stake in explaining the truth about Washington's real aims and in mobilizing the weightiest possible social forces to oppose the impending war.

These are the facts documented and discussed in this book.

In only fourteen weeks, between the beginning of August and early November 1990, the U.S. government has organized the deployment, from the United States and allied governments, of nearly half a million troops, including many heavy armored divisions. These invasion forces are poised on the borders of Iraq and Kuwait. The Pentagon boasts that this has been the speediest operation of its size in the history of warfare. It represents Washington's largest military mobilization since the Vietnam War. It is Britain's biggest military operation since the war against Argentina in 1982 to seize the Malvinas Islands. It is the largest French government mobilization since the Algerian war in the 1950s and early 1960s. The armies, navies, and air forces ready to launch an assault against the Iraqi people are equipped with the most modern tanks, attack helicopters, fighter planes, bombers, and battleships, and are supported by the newest and heaviest guns in the U.S. and other imperialist arsenals.

The military buildup, however, is far from complete. To better prepare for devastating military action against Iraq, U.S. combat forces on the front lines in Saudi Arabia will be doubled in coming weeks, bringing massive new quantities of war matériel with them. Combat reserve units have been called to active duty, and the Pentagon has announced that no troops will be rotated out of their battle stations in the Middle East.

In their preparations for war, the U.S. rulers have marshaled a coalition of some thirty governments to send military units to participate in what they present as a United Nations–endorsed joint operation. In addition to the United States, ground troops have been committed by Argentina, Bahrain, Bangladesh, Britain, Canada, Czechoslovakia, Egypt, France, Kuwait, Morocco, Oman, Pakistan, Qatar, Saudi Arabia, Senegal, Syria, Turkey, and the United Arab Emirates. Eleven other countries have sent naval forces: Australia, Belgium, Denmark, Greece, Italy, the Netherlands, Norway, Poland, Portugal, the Soviet Union, and Spain.

The stated goal of this military force is the immediate withdrawal of Iraqi troops from Kuwait and the return of the Kuwaiti monarch to his throne. Washington's true strategic objective, however, has become clearer with each passing day. The desired prize is an Iraqi protectorate, beholden to the U.S. government and the oil interests it represents.

Before a single shot has been fired, the human toll is already mounting. Body bags have begun coming home to the United States carrying victims of military accidents, while stocks of coffins and mortuary equipment are being flown to the Mideast on U.S. transport planes. Hundreds of thousands of refugees from Third World countries have been turned into pawns by Washington's callous moves as malnutrition, illness, and deaths have mounted. Soaring oil prices are devastating the debt-burdened economies of Africa, Asia, the Pacific, and Latin America. The slide of the industrialized capitalist countries toward a deep recession is being reinforced.

This war drive and its results are being orchestrated by the bipartisan government of the United States. But the people in whose name this is being done—those whose economic livelihoods will be devastated and whose sons and daughters will die in combat—have no say. No political party of working people sits in Congress, and no mechanism gives citizens of the United States—in or out of uniform—the right to debate the issues and vote on a declaration of war. That prerogative is reserved to the representatives of the twin imperialist parties that control the Congress and White House. After much argument and debate over tactical alternatives—and unanimous protestations of a desire for peace—those same parties have already dragged the people of the United States into four horrendous world wars this century: in 1917, 1941, 1950, and 1964. They are on the verge of doing it again, with all the unspeakable consequences it will entail in the Mideast and in the United States itself.

As Washington has accelerated its war drive, it has also orchestrated a political campaign to prepare U.S. and world public opinion for the bloody onslaught against the people of Iraq. The UN Security Council, as the following pages document, has been a central arena of confrontation in Washington's propaganda offensive.

Every resolution initiated by the U.S. government to justify its war moves has been unanimously backed by the five permanent members of the United Nations Security Council: Britain, China, France, and the Soviet Union, as well as the United States. The government of Cuba, however, now serving a two-year term on the Security Council, has been the sole voice in the United Nations to speak out clearly and consistently against the administration's war preparations, which are backed by the bipartisan Democratic and Republican coalition in Congress.

While U.S. president George Bush proclaims to the world that since August 2 "the peacekeeping function of the United Nations has indeed been rejuvenated by the actions of the Security Council," the Cuban delegation to the United Nations has been documenting that the opposite is true. In addition to a helpful chronology that details day by day the war preparations, the book contains each resolution adopted by the UN Security Council on the Iraq-Kuwait crisis, together with the statements related to these measures by Cuban president Fidel Castro and Cuba's permanent representative to the UN, Ricardo Alarcón.

Week by week, as events have unfolded, the pretexts and rationalizations for Washington's war moves have been exposed and rebutted by Cuba in the Security Council debates. Coverage of speeches by the U.S. delegation to the United Nations and by the Bush administration have been aired on U.S. television every morning and evening and featured as front-page news in the daily papers. Given Washington's thirty-year record of aggressive hostility toward the Cuban revolution, however, it comes as no surprise that Cuba's concrete and reasoned arguments have rarely been reported in the U.S. mass media.

That is what makes this book so useful. It helps arm those concerned about the march toward war with the facts, historical perspective, and international context they need to convince others and mobilize the broadest possible opposition to the slaughter Washington is preparing.

'Independence, sovereignty, territorial integrity'

In his remarks to the August 6, 1990, session of the Security Council, Alarcón emphasized Cuba's commitment to "the principles of noninterference in the internal affairs of states, no matter what the reason may be; of the nonuse of force in international relations; of the peaceful settlement of disputes between states; and of respect for the independence, sovereignty, and territorial integrity of all nations."

Based on those principles, Cuba voted August 2 in favor of the Security Council resolution condemning the Iraqi invasion of Kuwait. Cuba also voted for subsequent resolutions opposing Iraq's annexation of Kuwait and insisting on the rights of citizens of other countries to freely leave Iraq and Kuwait. On each occasion, Cuba used the opportunity to lay bare the facts surrounding Washington's aggressive actions and the hypocrisy of its newfound principles.

Cuba refused to vote for economic sanctions against Iraq, to endorse military steps to force compliance with the trade embargo, or to demand war reparations from the Iraqi people. Cuba denounced as inhuman—and as an unconscionable violation of fundamental human rights—the measures denying food and medicine to the people living in Iraq and Kuwait. Cuba was the only member of the Security Council to vote "no" on the air embargo of Iraq.

"Is the defense of the legitimate interests of the Kuwaiti government really the concern that has led the United States delegation to act as it is doing now," Alarcón asked the Council on August 6, "or is it the ambition of the United States to intervene in and dominate the Middle East?"

If Iraq is to be condemned for invading Kuwait, what about the U.S. invasion of Panama in 1989? Of Grenada in 1983? Of the Dominican Republic in 1965?

United Nations and United States

"Since the United Nations was born," Ambassador Alarcón told the Security Council August 9, 1990, "we have seen how certain great powers have sought to use the Council as a tool for their own strategic interests rather than as a body working for the maintenance of international peace and security." In the pages that follow, the truth of that assertion is well documented.

The UN General Assembly, in which each member country has an equal vote, has no powers to implement resolutions it adopts. The fifteen-member Security Council, in which the UN's executive powers are vested, operates on the basis of what Fidel Castro calls the "anachronistic, unfair, and undemocratic veto privilege." Each of the Council's five permanent members can veto any proposal that comes before the body. Nonpermanent members have no veto power.

As a result of this reactionary structure, Cuban leaders have often pointed out, the large majority of the nations and peoples of the world are effectively disenfranchised in the United Nations. "The Third World as a whole has a population of not less than four billion," Castro told a gathering in Havana on January 4, 1989, "and their most sacred interests, aspirations, or hopes can be frustrated simply by the veto of any of the five permanent members of the Security Council."

Or, it can be added, by their unanimous acquiescence.

History has shown that the veto privilege means the Security Council can only act if the United States deems the action to be compatible with its strategic interests. Washington has great leverage to pressure the Security Council to selectively apply whatever "fundamental principles" fit its needs at any time.

The U.S. delegation, like Cuba's, for example, voted in favor of resolutions calling for a halt to the Iraqi government's hostile actions against embassies and diplomatic personnel in Kuwait, as well as to the use of foreign citizens as hostages. As Cuban representatives noted, however, Washington's own record underscores the self-serving character of its vote. From the internment of U.S. citizens of Japanese descent during World War II, to the acts of violence against diplomatic missions and personnel by U.S. invading forces in Panama less than a year ago, Washington has often found it convenient to ignore the human rights and international treaties it today condemns Iraq for violating.

The U.S. government and its imperialist allies went to extraordinary lengths to organize UN-authorized airlifts so many of their citizens caught in Iraq or Kuwait could return home rapidly. When the Indian and other governments sought to send food to hundreds of thousands of overseas oil-field workers left without a livelihood, however, there was callous indifference to the plight of these people who, in Alarcón's words, were from "the Third World rather than the world of riches."

The Cuban delegation has also put a spotlight on Washington's brazen double standard with regard to UN-imposed trade sanctions. The UN has imposed embargoes on only two other countries in its forty-five-year history—in 1967 against the racist regime that ruled Southern Rhodesia (today Zimbabwe), and an arms embargo against the apartheid regime of South Africa. As Alarcón documented in his remarks to the Security Council on September 13, 1990, the U.S. government flagrantly defied the embargo against Southern Rhodesia, citing "national security" interests and the unavailability of chromium at a cheaper price elsewhere! Washington and other imperialist powers make their own unilateral exceptions in the case of South Africa as well.

Despite the near universal condemnation of Israel by the General Assembly for its invasion and twenty-three-year occupation of the Gaza Strip, West Bank, Golan Heights, and East Jerusalem, Alarcón noted on August 6, "there seems to be no need to impose sanctions against the occupier when it is Israel." When part of Angola was occupied by South Africa for some fifteen years, the Security Council again took no action.

During the Security Council debate on August 6, Alarcón asked whether anyone present really believed that what the U.S. government is doing in the Middle East "is the expression of a change, of something new in international life."

The history of the Korean War, and the UN role in that conflict, is particularly instructive. Forty years ago Washington used UN cover to organize what was in fact a U.S. invasion of Korea to maintain the partition of that country, in violation of the national rights of the Korean people. The division had been established by joint agreement of the U.S. and Soviet governments at the end of World War II.

In 1950, in a series of resolutions pushed through the Security Council by the U.S. delegation, the United Nations lent its authority to one of the largest military operations ever conducted by Washington. The entire 1950-53 Korean War was fought under the UN flag, while the U.S. government was authorized by the Security Council to command the forces dispatched to Korea from sixteen countries. Today the blue flag of the United Nations still flies over U.S. troops stationed along the border that divides Korea—despite a 1975 General Assembly resolution calling for dissolution of the so-called UN Command. The United States government refuses to this day to sign a treaty ending the state of war.

The legitimacy of the 1950 Security Council resolutions has always been denied by the Soviet Union and numerous other UN members, since these measures were adopted without the participation of either the Soviet delegation or that of the People's Republic of China. At the time, the Soviet government was boycotting the Security Council to protest the UN's refusal—at Washington's insistence—to seat the People's Republic as China's representative (Taiwan held the seat until 1971).

Washington's course during the Korean War, however, offers convincing testimony that U.S. actions in the Middle East today—including use of the Security Council to give international cover to U.S. aggression while assuring that no United Nations body has any say in U.S. military decisions—represent nothing new.

An end to plunder

In the Security Council debate on October 29, 1990, Alarcón noted that while the U.S. delegation kept the body diverted in metaphysical disquisitions over preambles and asterisks, "the government of the United States was announcing the dispatch of another 100,000 soldiers to the region we are discussing. At the same time the leaders of the U.S. administration and Congress were openly discussing how to begin the military attack."

This smokescreen has been thrown up not only in the chambers of the United Nations, but around the world. Washington's apologists are working overtime to deflect attention from the only facts that count: the massive size and deadly character of the imperialist-led military force being systematically assembled and readied to take the offensive.

For working people in the United States and around the world, the stakes posed by the war and economic catastrophe Washington is pushing us toward are very high. A U.S. war against Iraq would result in carnage for Iraqi civilians and soldiers, heavy losses among Kuwaiti residents, and the deaths of thousands of young workers and farmers wearing the uniforms of the U.S. and allied armed forces. It would bring untold economic hardship for hundreds of millions of working people. As Castro warns in the September 28, 1990, speech that concludes this collection, the consequences would be especially devastating in the Third World.

The broad international reaction to Israel's massacre of twenty-one Palestinians in Jerusalem, October 8, 1990, demonstrated the precariousness of Washington's position, however. To maintain its coalition against Iraq, the U.S. government was compelled to join in the condemnation of its main ally in the Middle East, the Israeli regime. American imperialism today acts not from a position of increasing strength but from one reflecting the growing instability and vulnerability of world capitalism.

A U.S. military assault on Iraq would generate worldwide revulsion. Massive opposition would erupt throughout the Arab world, other parts of the Middle East, and among Muslim peoples everywhere. An international protest movement would develop much more rapidly, and with more powerful social forces, than even during the Vietnam War. The first contingents of an antiwar movement have already begun organizing inside the United States. This was evident in the streets of cities across the country on October 20, 1990, when tens of thousands joined in actions calling for "U.S. troops out of the Mideast now!" The participation of a number of reservists and active-duty military personnel opposed to the war preparations in the Mideast was a harbinger of the deep-going opposition that will build up and eventually explode under war conditions.

Mobilizing world public opinion—and U.S. public opinion in particular—as a counterweight to Washington's drive toward a war is the goal of all those concerned about the future of humanity. That is why the role that the representatives of the Cuban government are playing in the United Nations Security Council today is important. As they have done before, leaders of the Cuban revolution are using the United Nations as a tribune from which to speak out and chart a course of action in defense of the interests of working people around the world.

In September 1960 Fidel Castro addressed the UN General Assembly. Pointing to the exploitation of the majority of peoples of the world by the capitalist rulers of a handful of countries, Castro told the delegates: "End the philosophy of plunder and the philosophy of war will be ended as well."

Four years later, another world leader, Ernesto Che Guevara, addressed the United Nations as head of Cuba's delegation. He cited Castro's statement and added: "But the philosophy of plunder has not only not been ended, it is stronger than ever."

When Castro addressed the General Assembly for a second time, in October 1979, he represented the Movement of Nonaligned Countries. He spoke, he said, "on behalf of the children of the world who do not even have a piece of bread."

"I have come to speak of peace and cooperation among the peoples," Castro said. "And I have come to warn that if we do not peacefully and wisely solve and eliminate the present injustices and inequalities, the future will be apocalyptic."

The pages that follow are a contribution to the battle to prevent the carnage and economic devastation that Washington is marching us toward, to prevent the future of which Castro spoke from becoming the present.

Mary-Alice Waters
November 9, 1990

1

'Is it really respect
for independence, sovereignty,
and territorial integrity
that motivates
the United States?'

Resolution 660 (1990)

SECURITY COUNCIL, AUGUST 2, 1990

The following resolution was adopted by a vote of 14-0-1, with Yemen abstaining.[1]

THE SECURITY COUNCIL,
ALARMED BY the invasion of Kuwait on August 2, 1990, by the military forces of Iraq,
DETERMINING that there exists a breach of international peace and security as regards the Iraqi invasion of Kuwait,
ACTING under articles 39 and 40 of the Charter of the United Nations:[2]

1. CONDEMNS the Iraqi invasion of Kuwait;
2. DEMANDS that Iraq withdraw immediately and unconditionally all its forces to the positions in which they were located on August 1, 1990;
3. CALLS UPON Iraq and Kuwait to begin immediately intensive negotiations for the resolution of their differences and supports all efforts in this regard, and especially those of the League of Arab States;[3]
4. DECIDES to meet again as necessary to consider further steps to ensure compliance with the present resolution.

'Cuba will work for a negotiated political solution'

FOREIGN MINISTRY OF CUBA, AUGUST 2, 1990

The following statement was issued in Havana.

At dawn today Iraqi troops entered the territory of the State of Kuwait following a halt in negotiations over their differences involving oil production quotas, the price of crude oil, and the demarcation of their borders.

Cuba views the use of force to solve international conflicts as unacceptable. In accordance with the resolution approved at dawn today by the Security Council, of which it is a member, Cuba stresses the urgent need to reestablish the sovereign rights of Kuwait and supports the search for a solution within the framework of the Arab League.

In addition, Cuba urges the international community to remain alert so that this action does not serve as a pretext for the government of the United States and some of its allies to increase their presence and launch a direct military intervention in the region.

Cuba, a nation maintaining friendly relations with Iraq, appeals to the government of Iraq to withdraw its troops from Kuwait, a country with which Cuba also maintains friendly ties, and to immediately resume the negotiations needed to resolve the differences by political means.

Cuba will initiate within the Movement of Nonaligned Countries,[4] to which both Iraq and Kuwait also belong, all appropriate contacts that can contribute to arriving at a negotiated political solution.

'We must not lose sight of the danger of an escalation of the U.S. military presence in the Middle East'

FIDEL CASTRO, AUGUST 2, 1990

The following letter to the chairman of the Movement of Nonaligned Countries was issued in Havana.

To Comrade Borislav Jovic
President of the Presidency of the
Socialist Federal Republic of Yugoslavia

Dear Comrade President:

I am writing to you in your capacity as chairman of the Movement of Nonaligned Countries concerning the regrettable events that occurred at dawn today between Iraq and the State of Kuwait, both members of our Movement.

We believe that the Nonaligned countries must not fail to exert their influence and act with a view to urgently bring about a peaceful solution to this conflict. We must keep in mind not simply the inadvisability of the use of force in international relations but also the possible consequences for the states in the region, including Kuwait and Iraq itself.

We must not lose sight of the danger—both for peace in the Gulf and for the independence and sovereignty of the countries in the region—that would be created by an escalation of the military presence of the United States and some of its allies in that area, or by the possibility of another attack by allies of the United States against—I repeat, against—the Arab states.

It is for these reasons that I urge you to take all the immediate steps necessary to have the Nonaligned Movement take action without the slightest delay in support of the efforts of the international community to attain a peaceful solution and to prevent the possible consequences I have mentioned.

In so doing, I convey to you the willingness of our government to fully participate in the actions decided upon.

Accept, Comrade President, the assurances of my deepest consideration.

Fidel Castro Ruz
President of the Council of State and
of the government of the Republic of Cuba

Resolution 661 (1990)

SECURITY COUNCIL, AUGUST 6, 1990

The following resolution was adopted by a vote of 13-0-2, with Cuba and Yemen abstaining.

THE SECURITY COUNCIL,

REAFFIRMING its Resolution 660 (1990) of August 2, 1990,

DEEPLY CONCERNED that that resolution has not been implemented and that the invasion by Iraq of Kuwait continues with further loss of human life and material destruction,

DETERMINED to bring the invasion and occupation of Kuwait by Iraq to an end and to restore the sovereignty, independence, and territorial integrity of Kuwait,

NOTING that the legitimate government of Kuwait has expressed its readiness to comply with Resolution 660 (1990),

MINDFUL of its responsibilities under the Charter of the United Nations for the maintenance of international peace and security,

AFFIRMING the inherent right of individual or collective self-defense, in response to the armed attack by Iraq against Kuwait, in accordance with Article 51 of the Charter,[5]
ACTING under Chapter 7 of the Charter of the United Nations:[6]
1. DETERMINES that Iraq so far has failed to comply with paragraph 2 of Resolution 660 (1990) and has usurped the authority of the legitimate government of Kuwait;
2. DECIDES, as a consequence, to take the following measures to secure compliance of Iraq with paragraph 2 of Resolution 660 (1990) and to restore the authority of the legitimate government of Kuwait;
3. DECIDES that all states shall prevent:
   (a) The import into their territories of all commodities and products originating in Iraq or Kuwait exported therefrom after the date of the present resolution;
   (b) Any activities by their nationals or in their territories which would promote or are calculated to promote the export or transshipment of any commodities or products from Iraq or Kuwait; and any dealings by their nationals or their flag vessels or in their territories in any commodities or products originating in Iraq or Kuwait and exported therefrom after the date of the present resolution, including in particular any transfer of funds to Iraq or Kuwait for the purposes of such activities or dealings;
   (c) The sale or supply by their nationals or from their territories or using their flag vessels of any commodities or products, including weapons or any other military equipment, whether or not originating in their territories but not including supplies intended strictly for medical purposes, and, in humanitarian circumstances, foodstuffs, to any person or body in Iraq or Kuwait or to any person or body for the purposes of any business carried on, in, or operated from Iraq or Kuwait, and any activities by their nationals or in their territories which promote or are calculated to promote such sale or supply of such commodities or products;
4. DECIDES that all states shall not make available to the government of Iraq or to any commercial, industrial, or public utility undertaking in Iraq or Kuwait, any funds or any other financial or economic resources and shall prevent their nationals and any persons within their territories from removing from their territories or otherwise making available to

that government or to any such undertaking any such funds or resources and from remitting any other funds to persons or bodies within Iraq or Kuwait, except payments exclusively for strictly medical or humanitarian purposes and, in humanitarian circumstances, foodstuffs;

5. CALLS UPON all states, including states nonmembers of the United Nations, to act strictly in accordance with the provisions of the present resolution notwithstanding any contract entered into or licence granted before the date of the present resolution;

6. DECIDES to establish, in accordance with rule 28 of the provisional rules of procedure of the Security Council, a committee of the Security Council consisting of all the members of the Council, to undertake the following tasks and to report on its work to the Council with its observations and recommendations:

(a) To examine the reports on the progress of the implementation of the present resolution which will be submitted by the secretary-general [Javier Pérez de Cuéllar];

(b) To seek from all states further information regarding the action taken by them concerning the effective implementation of the provisions laid down in the present resolution;

7. CALLS UPON all states to cooperate fully with the committee in the fulfillment of its task, including supplying such information as may be sought by the committee in pursuance of the present resolution;

8. REQUESTS the secretary-general to provide all necessary assistance to the committee and to make the necessary arrangements in the Secretariat for the purpose;

9. DECIDES that, notwithstanding paragraphs 4 through 8 above, nothing in the present resolution shall prohibit assistance to the legitimate government of Kuwait, and CALLS UPON all states:

(a) To take appropriate measures to protect assets of the legitimate government of Kuwait and its agencies;

(b) Not to recognize any regime set up by the occupying power;

10. REQUESTS the secretary-general to report to the Council on the progress of the implementation of the present resolution, the first report to be submitted within thirty days;

11. DECIDES to keep this item on its agenda and to continue its efforts to put an early end to the invasion by Iraq.

'This resolution will be used by the United States to intensify its intervention'

RICARDO ALARCON, AUGUST 6, 1990

The following remarks by Cuba's UN ambassador were made during the discussion of Security Council Resolution 661 (1990).

At the outset, I would like to congratulate you on your work as president of the Council and to express our appreciation to your predecessor, the representative of Malaysia, for the way in which he carried out similar tasks last month.[7]

To Cuba, the principles of noninterference in the internal affairs of states, no matter what the reason may be; of the nonuse of force in international relations; of the peaceful settlement of disputes between states; and of respect for the independence, sovereignty, and territorial integrity of all nations are essential principles of international order. It is in defense of these principles that we have expressed our disapproval and condemnation of the entry of Iraqi forces into the territory of Kuwait a few days ago, and have declared that this state of affairs must be ended through the withdrawal of Iraqi forces from Kuwaiti territory and the full restoration of Kuwait's sovereignty.

As far as we are concerned, these are two states and two governments with which we continue to maintain relations of friendship that cause us to feel particular concern at the situation that has arisen between them. That is why my delegation cast its vote in favor of Security Council Resolution 660 (1990). Nevertheless, my delegation wishes to explain the reasons why it is unable to support the draft resolution now before the Council.

First of all, it seems to us that far from helping to settle the conflict, this resolution and the imposition of the sanctions proposed now would instead tend to complicate the situation even more at a time when Iraq has begun withdrawing its troops, as the representative of that country has reaffirmed here. Similarly, the draft resolution would facilitate the interventionist actions that are taking place in the region and are being openly promoted and proclaimed by the U.S. government. The draft would also impede the current actions and efforts of the Arab states to arrive at a solution.

Furthermore, the draft resolution suffers from other defects that my delegation feels obliged to mention. To begin with, we are asked to approve specific sanctions that have already been imposed unilaterally by the principal developed powers of the world. We are also presented with a situation in which a number of states—particularly the main promoter of the draft, the United States of America—seem to have suddenly discovered the value of those fundamental principles that I mentioned a few minutes ago.

Reference is frequently made in our debates to the changes taking place in the international arena. I wonder whether anyone really believes that what we have here is also the expression of a change, of something new in international life. Is the United States really concerned with defending the rights of weak states, of small countries? Is this really a defense of the principle of nonintervention? Are we really talking about defense of the principle of the nonuse of force in international relations? Is it really the need to promote respect for the independence, sovereignty, and territorial integrity of states that motivates the United States to urge these sanctions against Iraq? Is that really the reason?

Is the defense of the legitimate interests of the Kuwaiti government really the concern that has led the U.S. delegation to act as it is doing now? Or is it the ambition of the United States to intervene in and dominate the Middle East? My delegation has no doubt as to what the answers to these questions would be, but the Council and the international community have no reason for any doubt in that regard either.

The draft resolution before us was originally received by all of us in an almost identical version when it was faxed to us from the U.S. Mission at 5:48 p.m. on Friday, August 3. An attempt is now being made to justify the actions it proposes on the grounds that Iraq has failed to carry out the withdrawal of its forces from Kuwaiti territory or by interpreting various statements made in Baghdad on Sunday [August 5] or what has been said here by the permanent representative of Iraq. But that is not the truth.

The plan to impose sanctions on Iraq actually existed before we entered this new phase of Security Council deliberations, at a time when no one even knew about the statement made by the Iraqi government, also on August 3, to the effect that it was going to begin to withdraw its troops from Kuwait. But apart from this, while we were discussing or negotiating or holding consultations on this draft resolution, the U.S. government sent a contingent of marines to the territory of Liberia.[8] I do not recall any consultations held on that subject. I am not aware of any Security Council resolution or request made by any group of states to invite U.S. marines to enter the territory of Liberia without permission. Yet there they are and, as the United States has said, there they will remain for as long as they consider necessary.

To justify this draft resolution, reference is now being made to the positions taken by various states or groups of states concerning this lamentable conflict between Iraq and Kuwait. But we cannot help recalling that for twenty-three years all the states of the region—Iraq, Kuwait, and all the other states—all the Non-aligned states and the General Assembly, almost unanimously, have condemned Israel's occupation of the territories we have come to describe, by diplomatic tradition, as the occupied territories. Apparently those territories can be occupied forever. There seems to be no need to impose sanctions against the occupier when it is Israel. Was any account taken of the opinions of the Nonaligned countries and the countries of the Middle Eastern region in order to propose more effective actions to compel Israel to withdraw its troops from the occupied territories and recognize the rights of that other Arab people, the people of Palestine?

But all of us also know that some six months ago this same Security Council considered in informal consultations a draft resolution on the latest developments with respect to the occupied territories. What did the Council do? Was it able to act? Why was it not able to act? Is there anybody who does not know the reason? We all know that it was the opposition of the U.S. delegation to even a declaration that the occupation was illegal, let alone to sanctions or to more effective measures against the occupying state.

The territory of Angola—part of it—was occupied for some fifteen years by the South African regime's troops.[9] My delegation does not recall any occasion when anybody discovered the principle of noninterference and respect for territorial integrity, let alone urged the imposition of effective sanctions upon South Africa to compel it to abandon Angolan territory.

The territory of Lebanon—or part of it—has been occupied by Israel for twelve years.[10] On the eve of this deplorable and regrettable conflict between Kuwait and Iraq, as we all know, the Council had to consider once again the situation concerning the United Nations force in southern Lebanon. We had to confine ourselves to renewing that force's mandate and to issuing a terse and carefully worded presidential declaration that made no reference to stiff sanctions against Israel, despite the fact that Israel, as the secretary-general's own report stated, is not complying with the relevant Security Council resolution, is not cooperating with the United Nations force in the area, and, even worse, is attacking it.

Worse still, we had to learn from the report that two Nepalese soldiers had lost their lives in unprovoked incidents. They were the victims of Israeli weapons. Since we did not adopt sanctions, did we at least express the Security Council's condemnation of that situation? Did we even state that we deplored the fact that after twelve years of the occupation of southern Lebanon, Israel still was not expressing any willingness to leave the territory? Did we even express concern? Was there any initiative faxed to our missions for an immediate meeting of the Council to adopt such decisions? Clearly that was not the case.

Seven months ago the territory of another small and weak country [Panama] was invaded by the military force of a great power and in a matter of hours that power, the United States, took possession of that country. There was one innovation in that case that was perhaps without precedent. A new government was installed, and perhaps for the first time in the world the president, the head of government, took the oath of office at a U.S. military base, naturally in the presence of the commanding general of the occupying forces.[11]

That happened seven months ago. There was, of course, no U.S. draft resolution calling for the imposition of sanctions against the United States. But beyond that—regrettably I must say this—there was likewise not much sentiment in favor of such a proposal among the other members of the Council, and consequently the Security Council did not even make a statement on the matter. The General Assembly did do so; on that occasion it adopted a resolution, and the vote showed that four of the countries sponsoring the draft resolution now before us voted against the General Assembly's resolution concerning the illegal U.S. invasion of Panamanian territory.[12]

It has been said by some in our consultations that our inability to adopt positions consistent with the defense of those principles in other cases should not make us fail to do so now. In other words, we should let the United States choose how, where, and when those principles should be applied. However, we are not talking about past history now. The Council can, if it wishes, adopt effective measures with respect to the power that continues to occupy the "occupied territories." The Council can take effective decisions concerning the power that continues to illegally occupy southern Lebanon, and of course against the power that continues to occupy Panama seven months after its invasion. Then, if there were the slightest intention of being consistent, we could begin here and now to rectify the contradiction that arises when, in a selective fashion, an attempt is made for the second time, as [U.S.] Ambassador [Thomas R.] Pickering has reminded us, to institute such drastic sanctions against a country.

I can recall another occasion that may be the one the representative of the United States was referring to: the decision taken by the Security Council concerning the illegal regime of Rhodesia when it unilaterally declared the independence of that territory, for the purpose, as we all remember, of preventing the people of Zimbabwe—who, fortunately, live in an independent, sovereign land today—from achieving genuine independence.

The authorities of the racist minority regime in Rhodesia took that unilateral decision in 1965. The General Assembly immediately adopted a resolution, with extensive support from the overwhelming majority of its members, calling for effective steps against this regime to restore legality and to make possible a genuine process of decolonization that would lead, as it eventually did, to independence.

When did the Security Council act? In October 1965, in November, in December? Did it act in less than forty-eight hours? Or did it wait days, or weeks, or months? Despite the fact that all the states in the region—the African countries—all the Nonaligned countries, and the overwhelming majority of the General Assembly were urging the Council to carry out its task and adopt effective measures against Rhodesia, the Security Council acted in 1967, two years after that attempt to deprive the people of Zimbabwe of their inalienable national rights.

My delegation has no doubt that the adoption of this draft resolution, far from helping to bring a speedy solution to this conflict—which we believe must be achieved through the withdrawal of Iraqi forces and the full restoration of Kuwait's sovereignty—will, we are convinced, serve or be used as part of the designs of the United States to intensify its intervention in a part of the world that it appears to regard as its own property.

I am grateful to Ambassador Pickering for something I think is quite illuminating. I listened very carefully to his statement, as I always do, and at the same time I was following the text of the press release circulated by the U.S. Mission and containing the text of his statement. There were a number of additional paragraphs, additional ideas, which he inserted during his statement. However, there was one phrase that he left out, a phrase that is in the press release but was not spoken by Ambassador Pickering. I can understand his reasons for not wanting to say it, and I am grateful to him for having spoken as he did.

The second paragraph on page 2 of the text circulated by the U.S. Mission contains a reference to Security Council Resolution 660 (1990). It then says that the Security Council must unequivocally establish today that the family of civilized nations will not tolerate such behavior, that is, the behavior of a state that, according to the text of the statement, fails to comply with the Council's decision. After this comes a phrase that disappeared from the statement as spoken by the representative of the United States. It is very short, containing just four words, and I shall quote it: "not here, not ever."

That phrase could not be uttered because it highlights the inconsistency and the unacceptable selectivity of the approach the United States adopts with respect to this resolution. The United States really is not in a position to have these principles applied not merely here but also there and everywhere, not merely today but always, without fail. The reasons for this are, I think, more than evident, and there is no need to belabor the point.

We are convinced that the draft resolution presented here does not really help to settle the conflict. Moreover, we believe it is based on an approach that should not be put forward by the international community, one that is motivated not by a desire to restore legality or to safeguard the legitimate rights of the government of Kuwait but by a desire to foster the strategic interests of a great power that considers itself the master of the Middle East.

For these reasons, my delegation cannot support this draft resolution.

2

'The United States
is looking
to invoke the UN Charter
to legitimize armed
intervention'

'We see preparations for a direct military intervention by the United States and its allies'

FIDEL CASTRO, AUGUST 7, 1990

The following message was sent to Arab heads of state.[13]

Your Excellency:

I am writing to you because I am deeply concerned about the events that are now threatening the Arab world and humanity.

I firmly believe that at this crucial time it is still possible for the leaders of the Arab nation to prevent the conflict that broke out between Iraq and Kuwait from leading to an adverse situation for the independence of many Arab states, to an economic catastrophe, and to a holocaust affecting a large portion of their peoples. Such is the threat, as we see it, caused by the growing and accelerated preparations for a direct military intervention by the United States and its allies. No less alarming is the evidence pointing to steps aimed at the creation, for the same interventionist purpose, of a multinational force whose composition reveals a new relationship of forces on a world scale against the interests of the Arab peoples.

In its current capacity as nonpermanent member of the Security Council, Cuba did not hesitate to cast its vote in favor of Resolution 660, adopted by the Council August 2. Not without pain and bitterness did we take that necessary and just step in line with our principled policy concerning the inadmissibility of resorting to force and military superiority to solve differences among countries, more so when what is involved here is a fratricidal confrontation between Third World peoples. With both Iraq and Kuwait we maintain bonds of respect and friendship, nurtured by the solidarity of Cuba with the Arab nation and the Palestinian people in the face of Israeli aggression and colonial expansion. Additionally, our historical cooperation in several fields with a number of Arab countries is well known.

These principles, as you no doubt understand, are very dear to Cuba, which is permanently threatened with aggression. At the same time, it is our conviction that if there is one thing we should do now, it is to refrain from adding fuel to the fire of war. And it is this conviction that determined our recent abstention in the case of a new Security Council draft resolution sponsored and zealously promoted by the United States [Resolution 661]. They want to impose, among other measures, a total economic embargo on Iraq—a step that in our opinion lessens the possibility of finding a peaceful solution. The United States and its closest allies are congratulating themselves on this new resolution, which creates ideal conditions for an escalation of the conflict and for the probable use of the most powerful war machinery on the planet. The unmistakable aim is to entrench their domination in the region.

To punish Iraq for its regrettable and unacceptable action in Kuwait is just a pretext for the United States. They are looking for an opening to invoke Article 42 of the UN Charter to legitimize armed intervention in the name of the international community.[14] This is the disaster we now face. And there is no one it can be more offensive to than the leaders of the Arab nation. For it is the same Security Council, acting unanimously with the exception of Yemen and Cuba, that by virtue of the U.S. veto proved incapable of condemning, much less establishing sanctions against, Israel for its forty-year occupation of Palestine and other Arab states. Thanks also to this anachronistic, unfair, and undemocratic veto privilege and its immoral use by the United States, it has not been possible for the Security Council to condemn Israeli genocide against the heroic *intifada*,[15] or the actions of the Zionist army that have caused the deaths of members of the UN forces themselves in Lebanon.

It would be naive and, above all, extremely dangerous to give even a minimum of credibility to the motivations the United States claims for playing a leading role in the crisis. With its customary experience in manipulating things, the varied and repeated use of pressure, the military capacity for rapid deployment, and its proven vocation for political opportunism, the U.S. mass media, diplomatic corps, and Pentagon have joined with their Western counterparts to take advantage of the just indignation that Iraq's action against Kuwait instilled in the international community. They are questioning, disqualifying, and blocking any alternative for a negotiated political solution that is not subordinated to their geopolitical interests, and are wasting no time in deriving as much advantage as they can from the current situation.

What won't the United States be capable of doing in a vital region such as this one unless they are stopped in time? On other occasions they showed no scruples and slapped the face of the international community by converting a tiny state like Grenada[16] and a country they had already practically occupied like Panama, into a shooting range for their most sophisticated weapons.

How can anyone fail to see the danger of the United States launching an adventure of this nature when it was capable of planning and launching an air raid against the home of the Libyan president after assuming, without its current backing, the role of international executioner?[17] Can any other conclusions be drawn in view of the landing of U.S. marines in Liberia just a few hours ago?

I am writing to you and to other Arab heads of state at this time in the name of the responsibility we all share as members of the Movement of Nonaligned Countries and of the Third World. In Cuba we have confronted mortal dangers, including the threat of nuclear extermination in October 1962.[18] We are quite well qualified to observe, anticipate, and calmly assess the most dramatic of circumstances. Neither fear nor alarmism is involved here.

It so happens, in this case, that the threat extends to all Third World peoples without exception, and to the most sensitive aspects of our economies, our security, and our independence.

The forces of regression and plunder will not be deterred by the consequences of a military intervention if, as the United States hopes, Arabs and Muslims are divided among themselves and bleeding each other dry. The resulting wounds would be so deep that they would require decades to heal. This war would cause widespread destruction in the infrastructure and economies of the Arab countries. They would be turned into the battleground for a war that would not be waged in Europe or the United States, but rather in the Arab-Persian Gulf.

This, in turn, would create an economic catastrophe for the entire Third World, whose interests ought, in all fairness, to be taken into account at this time. It would be hard to imagine the extent of hardship and exhaustion this would create for the already battered underdeveloped economies. Oil prices would spiral out of reach for most of these countries, which are already devoid of fuel reserves or the resources to obtain them.

It is impossible to overlook, Your Excellency, the tragic irony involved if the United States and its allies in this inglorious crusade fulfill their goals—among them the consolidation of Zionist domination—with a minimum loss of life for the West.

Their plans, all worked out and tested over time, call for high-technology warfare, based on the supremacy of their weapons and know-how. The casualties will be mostly sustained by Arab armies and the population involved in the operation.

Let me share with you, Your Excellency, the certainty that inspires me of the wisdom and courage of the leaders of the Arab nation, and the vitality of its institutions.

Nothing and no one can replace this strength, this authority, and this morale in the immediate search for a negotiated solution to a conflict between two Arab peoples. Such a solution would, of course, include the withdrawal of Iraqi troops and the full restoration of Kuwait's sovereignty, without catastrophic war, immolation of peoples, and vast material destruction. In the same manner, I believe that the Movement of Nonaligned Countries and the United Nations system, with all its flaws and limitations, can buttress the united will of the Arab nation and help it to prevail against intervention and aggression.

The seriousness and dangers of the present situation demand rapid and effective actions by the most prestigious and outstanding leaders of the Arab world. The experience of history more than attests to how dominant powers like the United States are accustomed to imposing accomplished facts and unleashing processes difficult to reverse.

With all due respect and consideration, I exhort you to act with the speed that the risks involved demand and within the shortest time possible, overlooking the differences that must now necessarily occupy a second place. I regard this unity of opinion and action as an urgent necessity.

Do not doubt even for a second that in this just and noble endeavor you can count on the support of the overwhelming majority of the international community and, naturally, on the modest cooperation of Cuba.

Fraternally,
Fidel Castro Ruz
President of the Council of State and
of the government of the Republic of Cuba

Resolution 662 (1990)

<u>SECURITY COUNCIL, AUGUST 9, 1990</u>

The following resolution was adopted by unanimous vote.

THE SECURITY COUNCIL,

RECALLING its resolutions 660 (1990) and 661 (1990),

GRAVELY ALARMED by the declaration by Iraq of a "comprehensive and eternal merger" with Kuwait,

DEMANDING, once again, that Iraq withdraw immediately and unconditionally all its forces to the positions in which they were located on August 1, 1990,

DETERMINED to bring the occupation of Kuwait by Iraq to an end and to restore the sovereignty, independence, and territorial integrity of Kuwait,

DETERMINED ALSO to restore the authority of the legitimate government of Kuwait:

1. DECIDES that annexation of Kuwait by Iraq under any form and whatever pretext has no legal validity, and is considered null and void;

2. CALLS UPON all states, international organizations, and specialized agencies not to recognize that annexation, and to refrain from any action or dealing that might be interpreted as an indirect recognition of the annexation;

3. FURTHER DEMANDS that Iraq rescind its actions purporting to annex Kuwait;

4. DECIDES to keep this item on its agenda and to continue its efforts to put an early end to the occupation.

'Certain great powers have sought to use the Council as a tool for their own strategic interests'

<u>RICARDO ALARCON, AUGUST 9, 1990</u>

The following remarks were made during the discussion of Security Council Resolution 662 (1990).

I will be brief, since I have in fact no real need to explain my delegation's vote. My delegation, when it was first consulted about this situation and the draft resolution, confirmed that we would have no objection to voting in favor of the draft resolution, since we agreed that this decision should be taken at any appropriate time by the Council.

However, I feel bound to make a number of comments, because I have heard reports that someone, for some unknown reason, is seeking to misinform public opinion and the representatives of other states who are members of the Council concerning a supposed Cuban action to prevent or delay the adoption of the draft resolution.

As members know, we indicated at informal consultations yesterday that we were ready to vote on the resolution, which we were sure would be adopted unanimously. What my delegation has in fact said in the consultations we have taken part in over the past few days since the adoption of Security Council Resolution 661 (1990) is something quite different. We were saying it before the [Iraqi government's August 8] announcement of the annexation of Kuwait, or even before the intention to do so was made public.

I feel duty-bound to repeat what I have felt obliged to repeat constantly: our profound conviction that the Security Council and the international community must act energetically and promptly to prevent the conflict from becoming exacerbated and from spreading. We cannot ignore the obvious fact that certain powers are taking unilateral measures that are not in accordance with the decisions taken by the Council and—as we noted at an earlier meeting—that do not accord with the desire to maintain the sovereignty or territorial integrity of Kuwait or any other state. Such measures simply correspond to the aim of these powers to dominate the Middle East.

One cannot justify war and interventionism in the Middle East on the basis of an arbitrary interpretation of the right to self-defense. The world did not come to an end with Mussolini, and the United Nations was born out of the ashes of fascism. And since the United Nations was born we have seen how certain great powers have sought to use the Council as a tool for their own strategic interests rather than as a body working for the maintenance of international peace and security.

I am not going to make a long statement at this point. The last time I spoke before the Council, I called to mind that not fifty or sixty years ago, but here and now, the Council has failed to take meaningful action on other problems that confront us. My delegation will continue to insist that the Council must reject any unilateral or selective approach designed solely to benefit certain great powers. I know that some delegations do not like names to be mentioned, but in this particular case I am talking especially about the United States of America.

Reference has been made, for example, to the importance of monitoring maritime transport routes so as to ensure that an economic and trade embargo is strictly applied. That is fine; my delegation is ready to wait until August 17.

I think we agreed that on August 17 we would hold the next meeting of the committee of the Security Council (which was created not last week but exactly thirteen years ago) entrusted with monitoring the implementation of the embargo (of arms, not trade) against the South African regime.

A few weeks ago we saw a document from a prestigious non-governmental organization indicating that more than one member of the United Nations and of the Security Council was failing to comply strictly with the provisions of that embargo.[19]

The idea has been mentioned of using the naval forces of certain states that have these means available and are willing to provide them, to contribute to ensuring that the committee on the South African arms embargo is able to work more effectively. We look forward to receiving proposals along these lines on August 17.

But I think that I should call the attention of all members to the fact that it is not of benefit to the immense majority of humanity to accept the imposition, as a practice of the United Nations, of these selective approaches based on the priorities of certain quarters.

We think—and this is the only point that we have been stressing constantly in the past few days of private consultations—that we must act when the headlines everywhere disclose and announce that there are some who are marching toward war, who are preparing for war, and who are making calculations about the consequences this could have for their forces or military means. We think that it would be very irresponsible of the Security Council not to take this fact into account and not to act and act immediately. This has nothing to do with the adoption of Resolution 662 (1990), which we voted in favor of.

I would stress that it is particularly important for us to keep in mind this serious and disturbing state of affairs in the Middle

East region because, at the same time, we have heard today news of something that we trust can open a door to hope and the solution of this deplorable conflict between Iraq and Kuwait and this grave situation prevailing in the region. I am referring to the summit meeting of the Arab states, which should be just getting under way in Cairo.[20]

In this respect, I should like to quote the following from a message sent yesterday by President Fidel Castro to all the heads of state of the Arab countries—a message that I had the honor of giving personally to Ambassador [Mohammed] Abulhasan [of Kuwait] for transmission to his government:

"Let me share with you, Your Excellency, the certainty that inspires me of the wisdom and courage of the leaders of the Arab nation, and the vitality of its institutions.

"Nothing and no one can replace this strength, this authority, and this morale in the immediate search for a negotiated solution to a conflict between two Arab peoples. Such a solution would, of course, include the withdrawal of Iraqi troops and the full restoration of Kuwait's sovereignty, without catastrophic war, immolation of peoples, and vast material destruction."

My delegation expresses the hope that given the concerted efforts of all the Arab states, they will be able to find a fair and swift solution to this conflict and thus shut the door in the face of the imperialists of today and yesterday, who are seeking to dominate the Middle East and treat it as if it were their own backyard.

'**Humanitarian concern should also apply to citizens of Iraq and Kuwait**'

Resolution 664 (1990)

SECURITY COUNCIL, AUGUST 18, 1990

The following resolution was adopted by unanimous vote.

THE SECURITY COUNCIL,

RECALLING the Iraqi invasion and purported annexation of Kuwait and resolutions 660, 661, and 662,

DEEPLY CONCERNED for the safety and well-being of third-state nationals in Iraq and Kuwait,

RECALLING the obligations of Iraq in this regard under international law,

WELCOMING the efforts of the secretary-general to pursue urgent consultations with the government of Iraq following the concern and anxiety expressed by the members of the Council on August 17, 1990,[21]

ACTING under Chapter 7 of the United Nations Charter:

1. DEMANDS that Iraq permit and facilitate the immediate departure from Kuwait and Iraq of the nationals of third countries and grant immediate and continuing access of consular officials to such nationals;
2. FURTHER DEMANDS that Iraq take no action to jeopardize the safety, security, or health of such nationals;
3. REAFFIRMS its decision in Resolution 662 (1990) that annexation of Kuwait by Iraq is null and void, and therefore demands that the government of Iraq rescind its orders for the closure of diplomatic and consular missions in Kuwait and the withdrawal of the immunity of their personnel, and refrain from any such actions in the future;
4. REQUESTS the secretary-general to report to the Council on compliance with this resolution at the earliest possible time.

'The Council should demand the U.S. end its illegal activities'

RICARDO ALARCON, AUGUST 18, 1990

The following remarks were made during the discussion of Security Council Resolution 664 (1990).

The Security Council has voted in favor of Resolution 664 (1990). Bearing in mind the views expressed by some members of our Council and Organization to the effect that the resolution is based on exclusively humanitarian considerations, Cuba voted in favor of it. My delegation naturally shares the concerns for the fate of any innocent civilian involved in the conflict.

We believe that it is legitimate to express this concern in regard to certain nationals of other countries who are currently on Iraqi and Kuwaiti territory. But we believe also that if there is a legitimate humanitarian concern, it should apply equally to the nationals of Iraq and Kuwait.

In light of these considerations, we voted in favor of the draft resolution. We are concerned about the situation of innocent people involved in any conflict. We are concerned about improper treatment of nationals of one or another country. We share this concern, which has been expressed by humanity on other occasions. It is not a new concern.

Indeed, not long ago in this country we were reminded of what had been done to persons of Japanese descent, who were interned in concentration camps merely because of their national origin and because the United States was involved in a war with Japan.[22]

We remember that much more recently severe limitations were placed on the ability of diplomats to leave Panama; what is more, tanks, heavy artillery, and major military concentrations were used to impede them from leaving their diplomatic missions and even moving from one embassy to another.

Although the situation was particularly grievous with regard to the diplomats of my country, we cannot complain of discrimination since similar treatment was meted out to the Papal Nuncio and his colleagues in the Vatican Mission in Panama, and to representatives of other countries that had nothing to do with the conflict.[23]

Having voted for the resolution, we are duty-bound, however, to draw attention to some of its aspects about which we have misgivings.

First, I quote paragraph 1 of the operative section of the resolution:

"Demands that Iraq permit and facilitate the immediate departure from Kuwait and Iraq of the nationals of third countries." In our informal consultations, references were made to the national origins of these individuals, and figures were given. But we have not yet received an answer to the question we have asked from the very outset: What is to happen to the large number of nationals of Palestine who are in the territory of Kuwait? Is the Council asking that they be permitted and assisted to return to their lands, which, as the Council well knows, have been illegally occupied for so many years?

Does the Council contemplate any action to ensure that the legitimate aspirations of the Palestinians, which predate the conflict with which we are now dealing, are fulfilled? Perhaps we shall have to wait a while to get an answer to that question, which from a statistical point of view seems to be rather important, according to the data with which we have been provided.

The resolution welcomes "the efforts of the secretary-general to pursue urgent consultations with the government of Iraq following the concern and anxiety expressed by . . . the Council [yesterday]."

But it was rather hasty to call on us to adopt this resolution that we have just adopted when, clearly, the secretary-general has had very little time to engage in these diplomatic efforts that we all want him to engage in.

In operative paragraph 2 the Council "further demands that Iraq take no action to jeopardize the safety, security, or health of such nationals."

We believe that neither Iraq nor anyone else should take any measures that will harm or jeopardize the security or health of these nationals or any other nationals in the area. It seems to us that this is a rather unilateral way of looking at the matter. Iraq is being asked to guarantee the health of foreign nationals on its territories, but we do not state in this resolution that the main factor that could place at risk the ability of the nationals of third countries or the nationals of Kuwait and Iraq to get sufficient food or medicine is that with the full knowledge of the Security Council, one power, a permanent member of the Council, has arrogated to itself the power to decide what goes into or out of the territory of Kuwait and Iraq.

The United States has not been authorized by anyone to halt the arrival of food and medicine to Iraq. Resolution 661 (1990), of which the United States was a sponsor, clearly excludes medicine from the embargo or the sanctions and recognizes that there must be humanitarian considerations with regard to food. Nowhere in that resolution is it stated that it is for the U.S. government to determine when there are humanitarian circumstances and when there are not. Nonetheless, we have now been informed unilaterally that from now on Washington will not take such requirements into account, and such products will not enter the area in question.

Hence, if the Security Council wishes to be the least bit objective, it should demand that the U.S. government put an immediate end to its illegal activities in the region. These activities, which have not been authorized by anyone, are adversely affecting the security and health of the nationals of various countries, including those of Iraq and Kuwait.

There have been other developments in recent days that, unfortunately, have not yet prompted the Security Council to take any action. Originally we were convened to consider the imposition of sanctions against Iraq, at a time when we all knew that such sanctions had already been applied by some developed countries. The Council adopted Resolution 661 (1990) and immediately—without any request from any quarter, without any authorization from anywhere—the U.S. government sent its navy, its air force, and its soldiers to the region and began to ensure implementation of the resolution. That is not only a violation of the Charter but a violation of Resolution 661 (1990) itself. And yet it is a resolution that the U.S. government is very much in favor of.

Subsequently, a de facto naval blockade was put into place. And barely forty-eight hours ago something rather strange happened: the members of the Council received a communication dated August 16, 1990, and sent by Ambassador [Alexander F.] Watson, at that time acting as head of the U.S. Mission. That communication informed us that the United States was applying blockade measures and alleged that it was doing so under Article 51 of the Charter and Security Council Resolution 661 (1990). I have already said that nowhere does that resolution authorize anyone or ask anyone—the United States or any other state—to implement the resolution by military means.

Article 51 is undoubtedly known to any "first-grader" in the United Nations system. It refers to a very old principle of humanity: the right to self-defense. And it could not be any clearer. It recognizes the right to self-defense but also adds, "until the Security Council has taken the measures necessary to maintain international peace and security."

What we are witnessing now is a new and interesting phenomenon, which should prompt the Council to take very clear decisions.

The Charter is being amended. We see a twisting of the terms of the original concept of the Charter with regard to self-defense. The Charter is being used, deceitfully, as something to be implemented unilaterally by one state after the Security Council has taken the decisions it deems appropriate. Does that mean that the United States is not really in agreement with Resolution 661 (1990), which it promoted? Does it believe that the Security Council has not taken the steps it should? Or, contrary to Article 51, does it feel that it has the right to infringe upon the authority and responsibility of the Security Council?

It has been alleged on other occasions—the U.S. delegation has used a variety of arguments—that the United States is implementing Resolution 661 (1990) on the basis of Article 41 of the Charter. But that article could not be clearer either. It refers to measures "not involving the use of armed force."[24] We believe that the Council will lose some of its credibility and moral authority if it refers only to some aspects of the complex and serious conflict with which we are dealing, and if it does so on the basis of a decision taken by one permanent member who then decides when we should be convened, for what purpose, and to discuss which part of a given conflict, in order to make a rapid decision on the matter.

Up to now the Security Council has been unable to act in another situation, one that is extremely clear, because one of its members is using the resolutions of the Security Council in the manner it deems most suitable to protect its own interests.

I have before me the text of an important statement, a message from a distinguished Arab leader, President Ben Ali of the Republic of Tunisia, to his people a few days ago. I shall read out part of the message, as follows:

"The situation makes us wonder with bitterness about the basis for invoking international legality as a pretext for sending foreign troops to Arab soil. We ourselves have put such legality to the test through the now chronic Palestinian matter, the occupation of Arab territories, the invasion of Lebanon, and the repression of the *intifada,* despite the many resolutions adopted by the United Nations and the many votes on behalf of those who are clamoring for their legitimate rights.

"Events have demonstrated that legality and the principles that supposedly back it up are not adequate in face of the vital interests of the major powers, and that this legality changes depending on those interests and their relations with the party to be condemned."

In expressing our agreement with that statement made by the president of the Republic of Tunisia, we should like once again to call the Council's attention to the need to take measures that will really make it possible to resolve the conflict peacefully. At the very least we should make sure that the Council's resolutions or decisions are implemented in the manner in which the Council itself decides.

My delegation voted in favor of the draft resolution out of humanitarian considerations, which we consider to be legitimate. Some of our colleagues have explained their concerns with regard to their own nationals in the region.

We also voted in favor of the draft resolution because we believe that it might, if the Council's authority is respected, help ensure that this aspect is not used as one more excuse not to seek peace but to continue along the course of war and military intervention.

The representative of the United States concluded his statement by saying something that may be quite normal, but that at the same time could be a terrible threat. He said the United States was not only supporting the draft resolution but would seek its full implementation. I am not quoting exactly, because the U.S. delegation did not circulate the text of the statement. Earlier, saying that it sought full implementation of sanctions, the United States sent in its navy and deployed major military units, which continue to move into the area. Now will the United States also implement this resolution by using force? Will it use the resolution to take unilateral measures, or will U.S. action be kept strictly within the parameters of this resolution, adopted unanimously? We shall wait and see.

'We cannot accept that a member of the Council manipulates the Council decisions'

RICARDO ALARCON, AUGUST 18, 1990

The following remarks were made in response to the comments of Thomas Pickering, the U.S. permanent representative to the United Nations.

Far be it from me at this stage to embark upon a legal discussion, but we still have the same concern. That is whether Article 51 can be construed to allow, on the decision of any member state, actions that have not been agreed upon by the Security Council, including the use of armed force, and whether Resolution 661 (1990) can be construed to allow the United States to use military means for a purpose no one has authorized. I think we are right to express our profound concern that the United States will also try to promote the "full implementation" of the resolution we have just adopted by taking aggressive military action, including the use of warships and bombers.

I think what is most important about the article and resolution from which he has quoted is that both assert this Council's authority to handle the crisis. Here we have a delegation that comes before us, as it frequently does, and calls upon us to take a decision so that the Council may act. Then it goes on to say it is acting as it must act, irrespective of the decisions of the Council.

Either one follows decisions of the Council or one does not. But we cannot accept that a member of the Council manipulates the Council's decisions according to its own interests.

The only special privilege of permanent members is the one unfortunately set forth in the Charter: the right of veto. But please; I think it would be a most serious matter for all members of the Organization if we were to tolerate their using the Charter and the decisions of the Council to do as they please.

4

'A grave violation
of the UN Charter
legitimizing illegal actions
by the U.S. Navy in the Gulf'

Resolution 665 (1990)

SECURITY COUNCIL, AUGUST 25, 1990

The following resolution was adopted by a vote of 13-0-2, with Cuba and Yemen abstaining.

THE SECURITY COUNCIL,

RECALLING its resolutions 660 (1990), 661 (1990), 662 (1990), and 664 (1990) and demanding their full and immediate implementation,

HAVING DECIDED in Resolution 661 (1990) to impose economic sanctions under Chapter 7 of the Charter of the United Nations,

DETERMINED to bring an end to the occupation of Kuwait by Iraq, which imperils the existence of a member state, and to restore the legitimate authority and the sovereignty, independence, and territorial integrity of Kuwait, which requires the speedy implementation of the above resolutions,

DEPLORING the loss of innocent life stemming from the Iraqi invasion of Kuwait and determined to prevent further such losses,

GRAVELY ALARMED that Iraq continues to refuse to comply with resolutions 660 (1990), 661 (1990), 662 (1990), and 664 (1990) and in particular at the conduct of the government of Iraq in using Iraqi flag vessels to export oil:

1. CALLS UPON those member states cooperating with the government of Kuwait which are deploying maritime forces to the area to use such measures commensurate to the specific circumstances as may be necessary under the authority of the Security Council to halt all inward and outward maritime shipping in order to inspect and verify their cargoes and destinations and to ensure strict implementation of the provisions related to such shipping laid down in Resolution 661 (1990);

2. INVITES member states accordingly to cooperate as may be necessary to ensure compliance with the provisions of Resolution 661 (1990) with maximum use of political and diplomatic measures, in accordance with paragraph 1 above;

3. REQUESTS all states to provide in accordance with the Charter such assistance as may be required by the states referred to in paragraph 1 of this resolution;

4. FURTHER REQUESTS the states concerned to coordinate their actions in pursuit of the above paragraphs of this resolution using, as appropriate, mechanisms of the Military Staff Committee,[25] and, after consultation with the secretary-general, to submit reports to the Security Council and its committee established under Resolution 661 (1990) to facilitate the monitoring of the implementation of this resolution;

5. DECIDES to remain actively seized of the matter.

'Blessings for the U.S. force already unilaterally deployed'

RICARDO ALARCON, AUGUST 25, 1990

The following remarks were made during the discussion of Security Council Resolution 665 (1990).

My delegation voted in favor of Resolution 660 (1990), thus expressing its support for the sovereignty, national independence, and territorial integrity of Kuwait and calling for the immediate withdrawal of the Iraqi troops that are occupying the territory of that state. It also voted in favor of Resolution 662 (1990), and in that way rejected the claim of annexation of Kuwait. In addition, it voted in favor of Resolution 664 (1990), thereby expressing its rejection of the situation that had been created with regard to foreigners in Kuwait and Iraq and the existing situation concerning diplomatic missions in Kuwait. Although we abstained in the voting on Resolution 661 (1990), my government has taken the relevant steps to ensure that our country too complies with it.

We are now being presented with a new draft resolution that raises a number of questions and compels us to raise various objections to it. While we recognize, as our colleague from Yemen has just done, the efforts which the original authors of the draft resolution have been prevailed upon to make and which have ensured that at least some formulations have become less ambiguous and less contrary to the Charter, I must state that the text in its present form remains unacceptable.

First of all, it is clear that the Council is now being called upon to take cognizance of something that has been going on for a few days. The Security Council has not yet determined that there is a need to resort to the use of military forces to implement any of its resolutions, but those forces are already deployed. The Security Council has not yet determined that the measures it previously decided upon have proved inadequate. The Council has not even been able—nor will be able, apparently—to wait until the secretary-general submits the first report on the implementation of Resolution 661 (1990), which, by agreement between the members of the Council, should be issued about September 6.

Apart from this haste to move on to the use of force, or rather, to permit the force already unilaterally deployed in the area to continue doing what it has been doing—now with the blessing of the Security Council—the Council is now to confirm that there exists in the zone a de facto situation that was not authorized by it, that was not decided upon by it, and that has nothing to do with the use of force in accordance with the Charter of the Organization.

In addition to the fact that the Security Council has not taken the stand it should have taken and called for putting an end to that situation—which threatens to aggravate still further the grave conflict we have been dealing with for some time—we are now being asked to endorse or validate an action that cannot be justified under law. Perhaps that is why it has been necessary to resort to a strange and tortuous wording that has nothing to do with the concepts laid down in our Charter and that specifically, in my delegation's view, represents a clear violation of Article 41; Article 42; Article 43, paragraph 1; Article 46; Article 47, paragraph 1; and Article 48, paragraph 1.[26] There will be very few paragraphs of Chapter 7 left inviolate if the Council adopts the draft resolution now before it.

Reference is made to using forces, but it is not known who the members of those forces are; we know it if we read the newspapers, but no one can know it from a reading of the draft resolution the Council is about to adopt. We do not know when the Council determined that certain countries would form part of those forces. Nor do we know who commands them, although all of us more or less suspect it is a ranking officer of the U.S. forces, identified every day as the chief of operations in the region.

But that commander has not been appointed by this Council, and if Chapter 7 of the UN Charter still remains in effect, it is the job of the Council to designate the officer to command the forces it decides to employ. According to operative paragraph 1, these forces will be operating in the area, but their purpose will be to halt all inward and outward shipping. It does not say where or from where; I assume it means the region. But it is so ill-defined that the zone could extend all around the planet.

Nor does it indicate against whom these forces would operate, although it is implied that the purpose would be to halt all—I emphasize "all"—maritime shipping, whether inward or outward. The text fails to stipulate to whom such forces would be responsible. It is clear they would be responsible to their immediate military commanders, but the Council is now taking on an ambiguous responsibility because the same operative paragraph states, although I don't know why, "under the authority of the Security Council."

If the Security Council is really acting responsibly and seriously—and those who are observing its work must assume at the very least that it is when it talks of using military force—then the Council should have drawn on those articles of Chapter 7 that clearly spell out how this responsibility, this authority, should be exercised.

For example, Article 46, which we presume is still valid because we are not aware that the Charter has been revised in these early hours of the morning, states:

"Plans for the application of armed force shall be made by the Security Council with the assistance of the Military Staff Committee."

It appears that tonight will mark the birth of the Military Staff Committee because there is a reference to it—for what I believe to be the first time—in operative paragraph 4 of a draft that will probably be approved. As far as I know, it has not been meeting to draft any plan, and I do not believe the Council has convened it either formally or informally to draw up any plan for the deployment of any forces in any part of the world.

The subsequent article, Article 47, in speaking of the functions of that committee, says among other things that it should assist the Security Council in the "employment and command of forces placed at its disposal." Article 43, which I suspect is also still valid, says that "All members of the United Nations, in order to contribute to the maintenance of international peace and security, undertake to make available to the Security Council, on its call. . . ."

The rest of the paragraph, which is quite long, spells out the special measures that must be undertaken to place at the disposal of the Security Council the armed forces it requests. Therefore one can imagine the steps the Security Council would have to take, should it determine that measures already taken under Article 41, which as yet excludes the use of force, were inadequate. It would first act in conformity with Article 42, without overlooking the articles that follow, and make a determination as to whether the measures on whose implementation the secretary-general would be reporting in two weeks had been insufficient. After having done that, it would then have to consider whether additional measures were necessary, possibly including the use of military forces. The Council would then request certain states to make some of those forces available to the Security Council. The Council would make the plans for the deployment and operations of those forces and would assume command of them.

However carefully and however often one reads the draft resolution that will soon be submitted to a vote, it is impossible to find any of these criteria in any of its paragraphs. In adopting this draft resolution, as I imagine the Council will do, the Council will in fact through its own resolution allow the continuation of an illegitimate situation. That situation will then assume a kind of legitimacy because of the adoption of this draft resolution, which I imagine will become Resolution 665 (1990).

We would all be deceiving ourselves if we thought that by giving a number to a set of unilateral actions and provisions they will cease being violations of the Charter and of the fundamental principles of the United Nations. We would be deceiving ourselves if we thought that by adding the UN insignia to some of the vessels in the zone, we would then be acting in accordance with Chapter 7 of the Charter. But in addition—and this is the most regrettable thing—we would perhaps be adding fuel and further reason for alarm to an already grave situation that is already a cause for great alarm and concern throughout the international community. That is, it is a matter of further alarm for the world to see this Council acting in a manner that departs from its fundamental functions.

There are some other questions that are even more difficult to answer, or even to imagine an answer to. The draft resolution refers to forces that have been deployed, specifically to maritime forces. Everyone is aware that there are also numerous forces on the ground and in the air, operating according to a plan that is unknown to any of us around this table except perhaps for our colleague from the United States. They are operating under a command structure that is also unknown to anyone except perhaps him. So there are naval, air, and land forces in the area, and they may be carrying out tasks in accordance with what the resolution calls for or they may add to the conflict in the region.

We can now anticipate that the Security Council will be required to take responsibility for any other action or warlike move that may arise from the decision of the commander of our forces, someone who up to now we neither know nor have designated. Is this really the way the Security Council should act on questions of such importance as the use of armed force to supposedly guarantee the implementation of decisions of this body?

We have had many long hours of discussion and negotiation, but we are truly very far from being convinced that this is the appropriate approach to be taken by this body or by the United Nations.

I should like to add, in conclusion, that my delegation continues to believe that no action or decision adopted or to be adopted by this Council can give it the political, legal, or moral authority to undertake any kind of action of an inherently inhuman character.

In this respect we refer to any action designed to deprive millions of innocent civilians—including children, women, and elderly people—of food, medicine, or medical assistance. My delegation firmly maintains this interpretation of international morality, of international legality, and no devious argument or attempt at justification can sway us from this conviction.

My delegation will not, of course, for the reasons I have stated, vote in favor of the draft resolution.

'Cuba refuses to legitimize the piratical actions of the U.S. Navy'

'GRANMA' EDITORIAL, AUGUST 27, 1990

The following editorial was published in the August 27, 1990, issue of Granma, *the daily newspaper of the Communist Party of Cuba.*

After a week of negotiations, the United States succeeded on Saturday [August 25] in having the Security Council adopt Resolution 665, a resolution that for the first time in the history of the United Nations authorizes the use of force to ensure compliance with an embargo—in this case, an embargo decreed against Iraq.

Cosponsors of the resolution included the United States, the United Kingdom, and France. Thirteen countries that are members of the Council voted for it, including the five permanent members (China, the United States, France, the United Kingdom, and the Soviet Union). Cuba and Yemen abstained.

The initial version of the resolution was first circulated Monday, August 20. In the course of negotiations that the U.S. representative conducted with other members of the Security Council, the draft underwent a number of modifications that softened its language but did not alter its essence. Retained in particular were sections that constitute a grave violation and unacceptable reinterpretation of the United Nations Charter, in effect giving legitimacy to the unilateral and illegal actions carried out by the U.S. Navy in the Gulf. This opens the door to further actions that may bring about an armed conflict with dangerous and unforeseeable consequences.

In assessing the issue, it is important to note that Security Council Resolution 661 of August 6, establishing the embargo against Iraq, is based on Chapter 7 of the UN Charter, in particular on Article 41 of Chapter 7, which deals with measures—sanctions—that do not involve the use of force. Resolution 661 also established a committee, chaired by Finland, to verify compliance with the resolution, and asked the secretary-general of the United Nations to provide the Security Council with a report on this aspect "within thirty days."

Up to now, however, neither the committee nor the secretary-general have presented a report indicating these measures are inadequate or that the embargo is not being complied with.

The document approved Saturday [August 25] by the Security Council establishes—without stating it—a de facto naval blockade of Iraq. But such a measure can be adopted only on the basis of Article 42 of the Charter (which authorizes the use of force). The fact that the Council's decision is not based on Article 42 not only undermines its validity but is a violation of the Charter itself.

What is the violation? It stems from the fact that a decision has been made to apply measures that involve the use of force, and that this has been done without first establishing that the steps taken so far within the context of Resolution 661 are inadequate and have been proven to be so. This action was taken not by invoking Article 42 of the Charter as is legally required, but by acting as if the new measures did not go beyond Article 41, which applies only to actions that do not involve the use of force.

This violation is a deceitful and unlawful reinterpretation of the UN Charter. It introduces grave provisions with dangerous consequences, under the cover of decisions whose scope stops

U.S. forces attacking a village during the Korean War of 1950-53. U.S. and allied troops waged that war under the UN flag, leaving two million people dead.

precisely short of the use of force.

Also of concern is the fact that the Council has decided to leave in the hands of a group of unidentified states (the resolution vaguely refers to "those member states cooperating with the government of Kuwait which are deploying maritime forces to the area") the authority to use "such measures commensurate to the specific circumstances as may be necessary under the authority of the Security Council to halt all inward and outward maritime shipping."

It is truly astounding that a body that has never before in the forty-five-year history of the United Nations authorized the use of force should do so now in such an irresponsible manner.[27] It has not even identified the governments that will implement it, the extent of their powers to do so, or who will decide on the degree of force "commensurate to the specific circumstances as may be necessary."

This is the context in which Cuba refused—despite Iraq's unacceptable conduct in invading and occupying Kuwait and in refusing to comply with the Security Council resolutions cited— to endorse such a violation and reinterpretation of the UN Charter and to legitimize by its vote the piratical actions the U.S. Navy has been carrying out in the Arab-Persian Gulf.

Cuba also believes that the United Nations secretary-general, the Security Council, the leaders of the Arab League and of the Nonaligned Movement can take actions that will help attain a political settlement and prevent a conflict of greater proportions, thus meeting the goals of the United Nations.

Resolution 665, adopted last Saturday, establishes a virtual naval blockade against Iraq that is without justification in the current situation. It gives U.S. naval officers the power to decide whether or not to use force and to what extent to do so. This is not only legally objectionable but also represents a military escalation that can only increase the tension. It makes it more difficult to attain a political settlement, which is what we would like to see and what the international community should be working toward.

5

'Access to basic foodstuffs and to adequate medical assistance is a fundamental human right'

Resolution submitted by Cuba

SEPTEMBER 12, 1990

The following resolution was rejected by the Security Council by a vote of 5 against (Britain, Canada, Finland, France, the United States), 3 for (China, Cuba, Yemen), and 7 abstentions (Colombia, Ethiopia, the Ivory Coast, Malaysia, Romania, the Soviet Union, and Zaire).

THE SECURITY COUNCIL,

REAFFIRMING its faith in fundamental human rights, in the dignity and worth of the human person, in the equal rights of men and women and of nations large and small,

RECALLING its resolutions 660 (1990), 661 (1990), 662 (1990), 664 (1990), and 665 (1990),

RECALLING FURTHER subparagraph (c) of paragraph 3, and paragraph 4 of Resolution 661 (1990), and deeply concerned about the safety and well-being of the civilian population and of the foreign residents in Iraq and Kuwait:

1. DECLARES that the access to basic foodstuffs and to adequate medical assistance is a fundamental human right to be protected under all circumstances;

2. DECIDES that in accordance with the above principle, under no circumstance shall actions be taken, including those resulting from the implementation of Security Council decisions such as resolutions 661 (1990) and 665 (1990), that may hinder access of the civilian population and the foreign nationals in Iraq and Kuwait to basic foodstuffs, medical supplies, and medical assistance;

3. REQUESTS the secretary-general to keep the Council permanently informed about the implementation of this resolution.

Resolution 666 (1990)

SECURITY COUNCIL, SEPTEMBER 13, 1990

The following resolution was adopted by a vote of 13-2-0, with Cuba and Yemen against.

THE SECURITY COUNCIL,

RECALLING its Resolution 661 (1990), paragraphs 3 (c) and 4 of which apply, except in humanitarian circumstances, to food-stuffs,

RECOGNIZING that circumstances may arise in which it will be necessary for foodstuffs to be supplied to the civilian population in Iraq or Kuwait in order to relieve human suffering,

NOTING that in this respect the committee established under paragraph 6 of that resolution has received communications from several member states,

EMPHASIZING that it is for the Security Council, alone or acting through the committee, to determine whether humanitarian circumstances have arisen,

DEEPLY CONCERNED that Iraq has failed to comply with its obligations under Security Council Resolution 664 (1990) in respect of the safety and well-being of third-state nationals, and reaffirming that Iraq retains full responsibility in this regard under international humanitarian law including, where applicable, the Fourth Geneva Convention,[28]

ACTING under Chapter 7 of the Charter of the United Nations:

1. DECIDES that in order to make the necessary determination whether or not for the purposes of paragraph 3 (c) and paragraph 4 of Resolution 661 (1990) humanitarian circumstances have arisen, the committee shall keep the situation regarding foodstuffs in Iraq and Kuwait under constant review;

2. EXPECTS Iraq to comply with its obligations under Security Council Resolution 664 (1990) in respect of third-state nationals and reaffirms that Iraq remains fully responsible for their safety and well-being in accordance with international humanitarian law including, where applicable, the Fourth Geneva Convention;

3. REQUESTS, for the purposes of paragraphs 1 and 2 of this resolution, that the secretary-general seek urgently, and on a continuing basis, information from relevant United Nations

and other appropriate humanitarian agencies and all other sources on the availability of food in Iraq and Kuwait, such information to be communicated by the secretary-general to the committee regularly;

4. REQUESTS FURTHER that in seeking and supplying such information particular attention will be paid to such categories of persons who might suffer specially, such as children under fifteen years of age, expectant mothers, maternity cases, the sick, and the elderly;

5. DECIDES that if the committee, after receiving the reports from the secretary-general, determines that circumstances have arisen in which there is an urgent humanitarian need to supply foodstuffs to Iraq or Kuwait in order to relieve human suffering, it will report promptly to the Council its decision as to how such need should be met;

6. DIRECTS the committee that in formulating its decisions it should bear in mind that foodstuffs should be provided through the United Nations in cooperation with the International Committee of the Red Cross or other appropriate humanitarian agencies and distributed by them or under their supervision in order to ensure that they reach the intended beneficiaries;

7. REQUESTS the secretary-general to use his good offices to facilitate the delivery and distribution of foodstuffs to Kuwait and Iraq in accordance with the provisions of this and other relevant resolutions;

8. RECALLS that Resolution 661 (1990) does not apply to supplies intended strictly for medical purposes, but in this connection recommends that medical supplies should be exported under the strict supervision of the government of the exporting state or by appropriate humanitarian agencies.

'Inhuman measures whose sole and exclusive victims will be innocent civilians'

RICARDO ALARCON, SEPTEMBER 13, 1990

The following remarks were made during the discussion of Security Council Resolution 666 (1990).

I wish first to congratulate you, Mr. President, on your assumption of the presidency of the Security Council for the month of September.[29] I wish also to congratulate the permanent representative of Romania on the way in which he conducted the complicated work that faced the Council last month. We also wish to welcome the new representative of the United Kingdom as he takes up his work in the Security Council.

Mr. President, my delegation is pleased to see you presiding over the Security Council not only because of your professional qualities as a diplomat, which will certainly contribute to our work, but also because you represent a country—the Union of Soviet Socialist Republics—that is united to mine by deep-seated ties of brotherhood and friendship. The Cuban people will be forever grateful to the Soviet people, to their government, and to their party for the cooperation they extended to us at the very beginning, when my country had to confront a ferocious and tenacious economic, trade, and financial blockade. That blockade has been in force for almost thirty years now. Of course, it includes a total denial of any possibility of access to the markets for food, medicine, or medical supplies in the country that is illegally imposing that blockade.

Thus, we are very familiar with the subject now before the Security Council. That is why we have various reasons for not being in agreement with the draft resolution submitted to the Council. Cuba regards as completely inadmissible the very idea of claiming that hunger can be used to deprive peoples of what is an absolutely fundamental right of every single human being in every part of the world and in any circumstance—that is, the right to receive adequate food and appropriate medical care.

We do not believe that anyone has the political, juridical, or moral authority to apply inhuman measures such as those whose sole and exclusive victims would be innocent civilians. And that is what we are concerned with here.

Moreover, we must recall that this draft resolution has been put before us in a concrete context. It has its own history. The Security Council was able to act expeditiously and with singular energy when it adopted sanctions against Iraq and Kuwait that were more comprehensive than any ever envisaged before. It acted equally hastily in adopting a resolution whose legality is at the very least open to question or, to be more accurate, a resolution that entirely violates the United Nations Charter. I refer to Resolution 665 (1990), which permits the continued exercise and deployment of military force in the Gulf region in an effort to impose, by force if necessary, the total sanctions that have been imposed against Iraq and Kuwait.

Resolution 661 (1990), on the other hand, at least contained reference to the possibility of providing food under humanitarian circumstances. Practically since the day it was adopted—or, to be more specific, since the establishment of the sanctions committee[30]—we have spent countless hours trying to define the criteria the Council should follow in interpreting these clauses of Resolution 661 (1990).

While that was occurring, the Council received information from various sources as to the consequences for thousands and thousands of innocent individuals. Affected first and foremost were the citizens of Kuwait, a country that has fallen victim to a situation we have condemned and rejected. We continue to call for an immediate solution to that situation. The Security Council has also punished—even more so now with these new measures—the people of Iraq and the nationals of many other states present on Iraqi or Kuwaiti territory.

Every day, in increasingly alarming terms, there are reports on the situation confronting the populations there. Even had we not been informed of this by the mass media, the Council has received more than one formal and official request for the adoption of urgent measures to keep people from dying for lack of food. We have read the letters from the ambassadors of India, Sri Lanka, the Philippines, and other countries. They have called upon this body, which was not compelled to adopt Resolution 661 (1990), to take humanitarian measures to deal with the situation in which these innocent persons find themselves. Not only has the Security Council not responded to those appeals; it is now invited to adopt a draft resolution that would basically make even more difficult and distant the possibility of even hoping that any real substance can be given to our supposedly humanitarian premises.

The draft resolution submitted to us does not explain what will happen to the 100,000 Sri Lankans who have been trapped on Kuwaiti territory, and no one has even suggested how they can receive food. The Security Council will now establish machinery that is neither swift nor compelling. It is not motivated by the anxiety and haste that caused us to spend so many nights in this chamber in August, but rather by exemplary patience and singular tranquility at a time when we are dealing with human suffering.

First of all, we would entrust the secretary-general with the urgent task of gathering information on the situation regarding the availability of food in Kuwait. And the secretary-general, as we all know, has reported to members of the Council on the difficulties the Organization is having in the field. He has reported that the Organization basically has no representatives there in a position to shoulder responsibilities, particularly those that would flow from this resolution.

On the basis of such information the committee could proceed to analyze the data with a view to determining whether or not there exist circumstances indicating it is of the utmost urgency that Iraq or Kuwait be given humanitarian aid. The result would be the production of a report, not food, and I expect that the report would then come to the Council. But nowhere in the resolution is there even a suggestion as to what this Council would do to find ways and means of ensuring help for the nationals of third countries and—please let us not forget—those of Kuwait, to whom no specific reference appears in the resolution we are invited to adopt—although it was clearly covered in the resolution the Council preferred to reject a few minutes ago. Nor, I repeat, is there mention of Iraqi citizens.

We might envisage that, beginning now, the Council would resume the spirit of those moments in August and begin taking up with pressing urgency these very serious problems now confronting so many innocent people. Frankly, I see no special reasons for feeling enthusiastic about that possibility, because this very Council has also received a series of urgent requests under Article 50 of the Charter,[31] asking us to adopt decisions that would help alleviate the serious problems confronting countries other than those we have mentioned. To date, the list includes ten member states of our Organization, with Jordan at the top of the list. The moment is drawing near in which we may be compelled to act at a pace even greater than the speed with which we acted in August.

Soon a month will have passed since the permanent representative of Jordan [Abdullah Salah], in a well-documented communication, told the Council about the very serious economic and social consequences the sanctions established in Resolution 661 (1990) would have on his country. If, after all this time, the Council was even able to do so much as adopt a resolution regarding Jordan—and it is not yet clear to my delegation that this is the case—we would finally be showing some kind of concern about the case we all acknowledge to be the most urgent and grave of all, the one that most of all ought to be dealt with speedily.

I am not in a position to say much that is encouraging to the nine other colleagues on the list, whose cases we have not yet even had a chance to consider. I believe this Council has a great moral responsibility. On the one hand, it is right that we should all try to ensure full implementation of the basic resolutions we have adopted—above all, in our opinion, Resolution 660 (1990), which calls for an end to the conflict in the region. It is also correct for us to monitor, through the sanctions committee, complete implementation of these measures as they were stipulated in the text of the resolution adopted here. But on the other hand, I also think the Council should act as a body that demonstrates maturity and a sense of responsibility.

The history of this Organization is perfectly well known. The hour is too late for me to take the Council through the lengthy list of countries that were represented here when the Council or the General Assembly discussed the question of economic sanctions in the past. Any case we might choose at random would clearly demonstrate that before the adoption of any decision there was painstaking care to take into consideration the economic consequences that decision might entail.

In certain cases, such as that of South Africa, there is an inexhaustible store of quotations from some permanent members of the Council, even very recent quotations—there is no need to go back into history—in which they argued that economic sanctions should not be imposed against South Africa because these would also harm the country's Black majority. I know that our colleagues from the United States and the United Kingdom are very familiar with that position, because it is one they consistently maintained for many years; they continue to maintain it to some extent.

Then there is the case of the economic sanctions that were imposed against Southern Rhodesia. At that time the United States—which is not a Third World country or a poor country, but a wealthy developed country—felt it had to violate them by continuing to import chromium from Southern Rhodesia. It stated as much right here, in the Security Council, in this very chamber. And the Council, as far as I know, sent no fleets, adopted no resolutions of condemnation, and took no special measures of any sort. It seemed to consider it natural that the representative of the United States should say something I am going to quote. It will be one of the few quotes I cite.

(*Speaks in English:*) "The United States representative explained that the decision to resume imports of Southern Rhodesian chromium had been prompted by genuine considerations of United States national security and by its requirements of materials of strategic importance which could not be obtained cheaper anywhere else."

(*Continues in Spanish:*) Can you imagine, fellow representatives, if any state in the world were today to apply the same logic to oil, for which we now have to pay at least double the price we were paying before this crisis? Isn't oil a strategic material for everyone? Hasn't this been explained clearly by the ten representatives who have communicated with the Council under Article 50 of the Charter? But in the document I quoted from—which is not something from ancient history—it seemed to be natural for a great power to tell the Security Council that it had decided to continue to buy chromium, despite the ban, because it could not find it cheaper elsewhere. Another quotation:

(*Speaks in English:*) "He pointed out the United States imports of strategic materials from Southern Rhodesia amounted to only 2 percent of the territory's total exports of those commodities."

(*Continues in Spanish:*) It was in 1972 that the then permanent representative of the United States [George Bush] told that to the Security Council. The Council adopted no special measures, and the import of chromium continued. The following year the representative of the United States again explained his country's position. This quotation is even shorter:

(*Speaks in English:*) "The United States representative objected to the fact that many speakers had singled out his government for blame as a violator of sanctions. He emphasized that although the United States had authorized the importation of chromium from Southern Rhodesia, such imports constituted only 5 percent of that territory's annual exports."

(*Continues in Spanish:*) One year it had been 2 percent; the following year it was 5 percent. Still, it was a figure that was more or less acceptable to the Council and the imports continued for as long as the U.S. government felt them advisable.

There are also many references I could cite on how the arms embargo against South Africa was handled. Shortly after the embargo was adopted by the Security Council, the representative of the same country explained why the United States continued to send arms to South Africa, and the explanation was apparently satisfactory at the time:

(*Speaks in English:*) "Current deliveries of arms to South Africa," he said, "consisted entirely of spare parts supplied under contracts made before December 31, 1963, the effective date of the United Nations embargo."

(*Continues in Spanish:*) Can you imagine what would take place in the sanctions committee if any country on earth dared say it was delivering exports to Iraq or Kuwait because the contracts were made before the date sanctions were adopted? I think the first to leap up and call this a clear violation of the sanctions would be the very country that was able to be so flexible when commercial advantages or contracts it felt must be respected were at stake.

I want to say that if this Council were in the future to deem it necessary to impose sanctions with the same strictness and firmness that have marked this case—for which there is no comparison in the Organization's history; the Council has never taken such action before—it should at least be obliged to foresee the consequences its decision might entail for other states that are not supposed to be the object of the sanctions. And it should be obliged to foresee the implication for millions of individuals who, simply because they live in the area of the conflict, could suffer grave consequences. If such foresight were impossible because the sanctions resolution had to be adopted within a few hours, the world might at least expect that in the course of the following month we would be able to adopt a consistent position on the problems arising from the implementation of our decisions.

My delegation considers that exactly the opposite has occurred. The Council has been compelled—for reasons that we all know, which I need not repeat here—to follow one course of action and one alone.

But something has occurred in the course of the past week that my delegation frankly finds irritating. I am revealing no secret here. I think that all of us in this building know what happened in the sanctions committee. We all know about the lengthy consultations that were held on the communications that had been received from the ambassadors of India and the Philippines on the one hand, and Sri Lanka on the other, about the efforts that should be made to take rapid steps, at least with regard to the specific requests we had received. And we all know how what began with a seemingly very simple discussion about whether or not we would authorize an Indian vessel to deliver food that was urgently required by the Indian population in the region ended up, by some strange twist of fate, with the resolution we have before us now.

That occurred despite the fact that the Council and its committee had precedents—not from ancient history but from the recent past—as to how such questions should be settled when they were raised not by Third World countries but by other states.

Everyone knows that when authorization was requested to fly the aircraft of some members of the Council to pick up nationals of their countries who wished to return to their country of origin, or to fly Iraqi airplanes to do the same, there were no long negotiations, lengthy discussions, or complicated texts. The sanctions committee quickly and simply expressed agreement to such operations. We did it once, and since then it has recurred without the committee having to discuss it again.[32]

My delegation entirely agrees with that interpretation of the request that was received at that time from the United Kingdom, if I am not mistaken. I expect that in carrying out such activities there had to be communication with the Iraqi authorities and there had to be some financial payments. It is normal to pay for the overflight, for airport services, and so forth.

But when India comes and tells us that tens of thousands of its nationals are in a distressing situation in which they lack food, and they tell us that they have a vessel that stands ready and loaded with food to send to Kuwait, we then become involved in the most complicated negotiations simply to authorize India to send one vessel to Kuwait one time to deliver food to those individuals.

Third World refugees from Iraq and Kuwait standing in line for food in the desert. They are victims of Washington's disregard for their plight. (Photo: Chris Cartter/Impact Visuals)

It would involve no financial transaction benefiting Iraq, but it might help save some innocent persons who have the right to live and who, by the way, have nothing to do with the parties in the conflict. I wonder whether it is really fair for us to be so painstaking with regard to the drama of people of the developed countries, the countries of the North, while we remain impassive before the clamor of hundreds of thousands of individuals whose names appear nowhere in the big newspapers, whose stories have not been told, but who, in the view of our delegation, have precisely the same rights as those from the wealthier countries, those with lighter skins, or those who bear passports that are obviously more useful.

At the very least, my delegation cannot accept having the Security Council act in such a differentiated and discriminatory fashion with regard to the various parties. We might have thought that one month later the Security Council would at least be in a position to deal with these problems and be responding to one or more of the cases of which we were notified. But instead we find something much worse. A draft resolution has been put before us that would in fact extend and reinforce the sanctions against Kuwait and Iraq to include food. That means our taking a tortuous path, one that in fact may be a dead end, with regard to imperative and urgent needs and requests received from various member states, needs that we ourselves know to exist.

It has been said on a previous occasion, as it may be now, that it is justifiable to take such drastic measures and be so cold, in the face of human suffering, in order to ensure that these measures are implemented and the goal attained—independently of whatever effectiveness we may have demonstrated in the past. But East Jerusalem has also been occupied and annexed by an occupying power. The Golan Heights was and continues to be annexed by an occupying power. This is not ancient history; it is a current fact. But there is no talk about that; there is no talk about sanctions; there is no talk of measures to force the occupier of those two territories, whose name is perfectly familiar to the members of the Council, to abide by the decisions of this same body.

I have quoted some material about South Africa. This is not ancient history either. At this very moment the General Assembly is considering a report from the secretary-general on the implementation of the declaration adopted by consensus only a few months ago.[33] At this very moment. This is not ancient history. Tomorrow the debate will continue here in this building, and as the secretary-general knows full well, his report contains information and replies from member states that certainly do not indicate they are complying or will continue to comply with the sanctions against South Africa. Rather what the General Assembly is facing today—and our African brothers and sisters know this full well—is a dangerous tendency to water down the policy of sanctions against South Africa, to try to undermine the position of the international community against apartheid, and to seek measures of accommodation with the Pretoria regime before the General Assembly and Security Council resolutions are complied with.

But it was also this very Council that established the committee to monitor the implementation of the sanctions adopted in Resolution 418 (1977),[34] and everyone knows that that committee has been sleeping the sleep of the righteous for approximately two months. Why? Because we had to concentrate on the real sanctions, sanctions there was a will to apply, sanctions that, come what may, will cost the lives that they will cost. We cannot accept this approach. And this is not ancient history. We believe that if we are to have a minimum of consistency we must consider the possibility of rescuing from almost certain death that other sanctions committee and that other set of partial sanctions, affecting weapons alone, that this Council decided on in the case of South Africa.

My delegation firmly believes that the conflict that has arisen through the invasion of Kuwait by Iraq must be settled by means of the immediate and unconditional withdrawal of Iraqi troops from Kuwait. We firmly believe that the full sovereignty, territorial integrity, and independence of Kuwait must be restored immediately. We believe that the nationals of third countries in Iraq or Kuwait have rights that no one should abrogate, limit, or infringe upon, such as the right to leave and return to their country, and the right to adequate food and to all other conditions inherent in maintaining their human dignity. But we also believe that these same rights are possessed by the people of Kuwait, the civilian population of Iraq, and the nationals of third countries in the region, despite the fact that those third countries have the ill fortune of belonging to the Third World rather than the world of riches.

We are not prepared to support any action that would continue to ignore the tragedy for which those who originally caused this conflict are responsible. But the Security Council is also responsible, because of the measures it adopted, and because in doing so it did not take into consideration the problems it was creating for innocent people.

That is why we put forward a draft resolution that we believed would receive the Council's approval. If you reread it, you will see that on the basis of quotations from the Charter of our Organization, it focuses on a principle that, while it did not receive the necessary votes, nonetheless continues to be a principle that no one has the right to flout: the principle that access to basic foodstuffs and to adequate medical assistance is a fundamental right to be protected under all circumstances.

Since it will henceforth be increasingly difficult for millions of innocent individuals to exercise that right, and since, far from mitigating the suffering of individuals—as is claimed in the draft resolution we are discussing—the Council's decision would instead perhaps increase it, my delegation is unable to vote in favor of the draft resolution that has been submitted.

6

'No reference is made to the need to find a peaceful solution to the conflict'

Resolution 667 (1990)

SECURITY COUNCIL, SEPTEMBER 16, 1990

The following resolution was adopted by unanimous vote.

THE SECURITY COUNCIL,

REAFFIRMING its resolutions 660 (1990), 662 (1990), 664 (1990), 665 (1990), and 666 (1990),

RECALLING the Vienna Conventions of April 18, 1961, on diplomatic relations and of April 24, 1963, on consular relations, to both of which Iraq is a party,

CONSIDERING that the decision of Iraq to order the closure of diplomatic and consular missions in Kuwait and to withdraw the immunity and privileges of these missions and their personnel is contrary to the decisions of the Security Council, the international conventions mentioned above, and international law,

DEEPLY CONCERNED that Iraq, notwithstanding the decisions of the Security Council and the provisions of the conventions mentioned above, has committed acts of violence against diplomatic missions and their personnel in Kuwait,

OUTRAGED at recent violations by Iraq of diplomatic premises in Kuwait and at the abduction of personnel enjoying diplomatic immunity and foreign nationals who were present in these premises,

CONSIDERING that the above actions by Iraq constitute aggressive acts and a flagrant violation of its international obligations, which strike at the root of the conduct of international relations in accordance with the Charter of the United Nations,

RECALLING that Iraq is fully responsible for any use of violence against foreign nationals or against any diplomatic or consular mission in Kuwait or its personnel,

DETERMINED to ensure respect for its decisions and for Article 25 of the Charter of the United Nations,[35]

FURTHER CONSIDERING that the grave nature of Iraq's actions, which constitute a new escalation of its violations of international law, obliges the Council not only to express its immediate reaction but also to consult urgently to take further concrete measures to ensure Iraq's compliance with the Council's resolutions,

ACTING under Chapter 7 of the Charter of the United Nations:

1. STRONGLY CONDEMNS aggressive acts perpetrated by Iraq against diplomatic premises and personnel in Kuwait, including the abduction of foreign nationals who were present in those premises;
2. DEMANDS the immediate release of those foreign nationals as well as all nationals mentioned in Resolution 664 (1990);
3. FURTHER DEMANDS that Iraq immediately and fully comply with its international obligations under resolutions 660 (1990), 662 (1990), and 664 (1990) of the Security Council, the Vienna Conventions on diplomatic and consular relations, and international law;
4. FURTHER DEMANDS that Iraq immediately protect the safety and well-being of diplomatic and consular personnel and premises in Kuwait and in Iraq and take no action to hinder the diplomatic and consular missions in the performance of their functions, including access to their nationals and the protection of their person and interests;
5. REMINDS all states that they are obliged to observe strictly resolutions 661 (1990), 662 (1990), 664 (1990), 665 (1990), and 666 (1990);
6. DECIDES to consult urgently to take further concrete measures as soon as possible, under Chapter 7 of the Charter, in response to Iraq's continued violation of the Charter, of resolutions of the Council, and of international law.

'Unacceptable actions in violation of the integrity of diplomatic premises and personnel'

RICARDO ALARCON, SEPTEMBER 16, 1990

The following remarks were made during the discussion of Security Council Resolution 667 (1990).

At the outset, my delegation wishes to express its appreciation to the delegation of France for the position it took in the negotiations that led to the resolution we have just adopted and for its willingness to seek compromise formulations that made it possible for all members of the Council to support the resolution we have just approved.

I must however say that, unfortunately, the resolution we have just adopted contains some elements on which I must comment. Above all, the text reaffirms some resolutions with respect to which our position is not changed by the vote we have just cast; this vote should not be interpreted as reflecting a change in our position. In our view, Resolution 665 (1990) violates the United Nations Charter. And Resolution 666 (1990), adopted only two days ago, contains approaches and criteria that are, in our judgment, of an inhuman character.

My delegation would have preferred different wording in some paragraphs of the text we have just adopted, where reference is made to aggressive acts. The wording here seems to us to be somewhat excessive; such expressions were not used even in Resolution 660 (1990), referring to the Iraqi invasion of Kuwait. We are also concerned about paragraph 6 of the operative section, since it might be inferred that some powers could use its provisions to exacerbate the conflict and press on to military action.

We regret that no reference is made in this text to the need to continue the efforts to find a peaceful solution to the conflict. We regret also that no space was found to mention the responsibility and function in connection with diplomatic missions in Kuwait that can and should devolve upon the secretary-general.

My delegation decided nevertheless to vote in favor of this resolution because we agree with the major elements of its operative part. We regard as absolutely unacceptable the actions in violation of the integrity of diplomatic premises and personnel in Kuwait.

For Cuba, respect for and full implementation of Security Council resolutions 662 (1990) and 664 (1990) remains an imperative necessity.

Our vote should also be understood as an expression of friendship and respect for France, Canada, and the other countries whose diplomatic personnel and missions have been and are the object of actions and incidents that Cuba can only reject.

'This resolution brings us closer to the outbreak of war'

Resolution 670 (1990)

SECURITY COUNCIL, SEPTEMBER 25, 1990

The following resolution was adopted by a vote of 14-1-0, with Cuba against.

THE SECURITY COUNCIL,

REAFFIRMING its resolutions 660 (1990), 661 (1990), 662 (1990), 664 (1990), 665 (1990), 666 (1990), and 667 (1990),

CONDEMNING Iraq's continued occupation of Kuwait, its failure to rescind its actions and end its purported annexation and its holding of third-state nationals against their will, in flagrant violation of resolutions 660 (1990), 662 (1990), 664 (1990), and 667 (1990) and of international humanitarian law,

CONDEMNING FURTHER the treatment by Iraqi forces of Kuwaiti nationals, including measures to force them to leave their own country and mistreatment of persons and property in Kuwait in violation of international law,

NOTING WITH GRAVE CONCERN the persistent attempts to evade the measures laid down in Resolution 661 (1990),

FURTHER NOTING that a number of states have limited the number of Iraqi diplomatic and consular officials in their countries and that others are planning to do so,

DETERMINED to ensure by all necessary means the strict and complete application of the measures laid down in Resolution 661 (1990),

DETERMINED to ensure respect for its decisions and the provisions of articles 25 and 48 of the Charter of the United Nations,[36]

AFFIRMING that any acts of the government of Iraq which are contrary to the above-mentioned resolutions or to articles 25 or 48 of the Charter of the United Nations, such as Decree No. 377 of the Revolutionary Command Council of Iraq of September 16, 1990, are null and void,

REAFFIRMING its determination to ensure compliance with Security Council resolutions by maximum use of political and diplomatic means,

WELCOMING the secretary-general's use of his good offices to advance a peaceful solution based on the relevant Security Council resolutions and noting with appreciation his continuing efforts to this end,

UNDERLINING to the government of Iraq that its continued failure to comply with the terms of resolutions 660 (1990), 661 (1990), 662 (1990), 664 (1990), 666 (1990), and 667 (1990) could lead to further serious action by the Council under the Charter of the United Nations, including under Chapter 7,

RECALLING the provisions of Article 103 of the Charter of the United Nations,[37]

ACTING under Chapter 7 of the Charter of the United Nations:

1: CALLS UPON all states to carry out their obligations to ensure strict and complete compliance with Resolution 661 (1990) and in particular paragraphs 3, 4, and 5 thereof;

2. CONFIRMS that Resolution 661 (1990) applies to all means of transport, including aircraft;

3. DECIDES that all states, notwithstanding the existence of any rights or obligations conferred or imposed by any international agreement or any contract entered into or any licence or permit granted before the date of the present resolution, shall deny permission to any aircraft to take off from their territory if the aircraft would carry any cargo to or from Iraq or Kuwait other than food in humanitarian circumstances, subject to authorization by the Council or the committee established by Resolution 661 (1990) and in accordance with Resolution 666 (1990), or supplies intended strictly for medical purposes or solely for UNIIMOG;[38]

4. DECIDES FURTHER that all states shall deny permission to any aircraft destined to land in Iraq or Kuwait, whatever its state of registration, to overfly its territory unless:

(a) The aircraft lands at an airfield designated by that state outside Iraq or Kuwait in order to permit its inspection to ensure that there is no cargo on board in violation of Resolution 661 (1990) or the present resolution, and for this purpose the aircraft may be detained for as long as necessary; or

(b) The particular flight has been approved by the committee established by Resolution 661 (1990); or

(c) The flight is certified by the United Nations as solely for the purposes of UNIIMOG;

5. DECIDES that each state shall take all necessary measures to ensure that any aircraft registered in its territory or operated by an operator who has his principal place of business or permanent residence in its territory complies with the provis-

ions of Resolution 661 (1990) and the present resolution;

6. DECIDES FURTHER that all states shall notify in a timely fashion the committee established by Resolution 661 (1990) of any flight between its territory and Iraq or Kuwait to which the requirement to land in paragraph 4 above does not apply, and the purpose for such a flight;

7. CALLS UPON all states to cooperate in taking such measures as may be necessary, consistent with international law, including the Chicago Convention,[39] to ensure the effective implementation of the provisions of Resolution 661 (1990) or the present resolution;

8. CALLS UPON all states to detain any ships of Iraqi registry which enter their ports and which are being or have been used in violation of Resolution 661 (1990), or to deny such ships entrance to their ports except in circumstances recognized under international law as necessary to safeguard human life;

9. REMINDS all states of their obligations under Resolution 661 (1990) with regard to the freezing of Iraqi assets, and the protection of the assets of the legitimate government of Kuwait and its agencies, located within their territory and to report to the committee established under Resolution 661 (1990) regarding those assets;

10. CALLS UPON all states to provide to the committee established by Resolution 661 (1990) information regarding the action taken by them to implement the provisions laid down in the present resolution;

11. AFFIRMS that the United Nations Organization, the specialized agencies and other international organizations in the United Nations system are required to take such measures as may be necessary to give effect to the terms of Resolution 661 (1990) and this resolution;

12. DECIDES to consider, in the event of evasion of the provisions of Resolution 661 (1990) or of the present resolution by a state or its nationals or through its territory, measures directed at the state in question to prevent such evasion;

13. REAFFIRMS that the Fourth Geneva Convention applies to Kuwait and that as a high contracting party to the convention Iraq is bound to comply fully with all its terms and in particular is liable under the convention in respect of the grave breaches committed by it, as are individuals who commit or order the commission of grave breaches.

'Some day the Council may devote time to efforts that will give peace a chance'

RICARDO ALARCON, SEPTEMBER 25, 1990

The following remarks were made during the discussion of Security Council Resolution 670 (1990).

First, I welcome you, Mr. President, and express my delegation's pleasure at seeing you, a distinguished Soviet personality, an outstanding leader of the government of the Soviet Union, with which my government has the most fraternal relations, guiding our Council's proceedings.[40]

The Security Council has shown unprecedented diligence ever since Iraq invaded Kuwait on August 2. It has adopted— sometimes in a matter of a few hours—an unending number of resolutions. For the first time in its history, it has demonstrated the will to enforce those resolutions.

Cuba voted in favor of the resolutions that rejected the inadmissible invasion of Kuwaiti territory, the illegal claim to annexation, the violation of diplomatic norms, and the conversion of foreign citizens into hostages. For reasons of principle, we reject the conduct of the government of Iraq in this respect and we appeal to it, once again, to cease such conduct and to abide by Security Council resolutions 660 (1990), 662 (1990), and 664 (1990).

We continue to believe that Iraqi troops must withdraw immediately and unconditionally from Kuwait and that respect must be shown for the sovereignty, national independence, and territorial integrity of that state. We reject any form of the use of force in an attempt to resolve international disputes.

Those principles, which are sacred to us and which we are all duty-bound to respect in the case of Kuwait no less than in the case of any other state, are basic to all peoples of the Third World. We consider it essential that they be respected as soon as possible in order to save the world—and especially the peoples of Asia, Africa, and Latin America—from possible catastrophe.

For those same reasons of principle, my delegation felt obliged on other occasions not to join with the rest of the Security Council. We believe the Council has a number of Charter obligations that it is bound to respect. Above all, we feel the

Council must be consistent. We do not think it has been consistent in the past or that it is being consistent now in light of its conduct on other cases. I shall not go into those cases, but shall mention only a few names familiar to all members: Palestine, Lebanon, apartheid, and Cyprus[41]—and there are many others.

But in addition we have lacked consistency in the decisions the Council itself has taken in haste since August. The Council, which has been deft and effective in adopting one resolution after another that we are all familiar with, has however been quite circumspect toward the growing calls from many states under Article 50 of the Charter. We have spent more than a month trying to find minimum agreement on this matter.

The Security Council has been inconsistent on the imposition of sanctions, which, I reiterate, are in the view of my delegation, inhuman actions because they deny thousands of innocent people, including children, the elderly, and women, a fundamental right no one has the authority to take away—the right to basic foods and to appropriate health care.

We have also been inconsistent in hastily adopting decisions without awaiting relevant information from the secretary-general. Actions have been undertaken or threatened in response to alleged violations of the economic embargo imposed on Iraq, when to date we have not received a single concrete accusation that the embargo is being ignored.

Now the Council is again being asked to state a position that would amount to strengthening the economic measures against Iraq without pausing to consider the adverse consequences this might entail for third parties. If these third parties later called on us to shoulder our responsibilities under Article 50 of the Charter, they might encounter only the more traditional Security Council, slow and circumspect about responding to requests from member states.

The draft resolution before us not only contains clear threats that other measures—military measures, I presume—will be used against Iraq. It also lashes out against any state that might disregard resolutions already adopted. To date, however, no information has been received to indicate that any party is doing so; we have never even considered an allegation to that effect.

Moreover—and this is the crux of the draft resolution—those measures would extend to international air communications between Iraq and other states in a manner that, in our view, has

Ricardo Alarcón, Cuba's UN ambassador, speaks to Security Council on U.S. war moves in Mideast. Behind him, Deputy Ambassador Carlos Zamora (left) and Counselor Abelardo Moreno of Cuba's UN mission. (Photo: United Nations)

very little to do with the charter signed in December 1944, in the midst of the war, to serve as the basis for the activities of the International Civil Aviation Organization (ICAO). It should come as no surprise that it was very hard to incorporate into the original draft resolution a specific reference to the December 1944 charter and its clear provisions.

My delegation views this text as continuing a line of thinking that, in our view, does not bring us closer to a settlement of the conflict. Instead it brings us closer to the outbreak of war.

I call attention to paragraph 13 of the text before us. It is unfortunate that the sponsors could not accept our request for a separate vote on that paragraph, which contains wording the permanent representative of Kuwait had been requesting of the Council since the beginning of the month. He rightly conveyed the anguish and concern of his government over the plight of the population of Kuwait under foreign occupation. Today— and in the context of a draft resolution that actually deals with another subject—the Council is finally showing some sensitivity, including sensitivity to the people of Kuwait, which, one would have thought, ought to have been at the center of our concerns. My delegation regrets that it will be impossible to put paragraph 13 to a separate vote; had this been done, my delegation would have voted in favor of it. We shall not vote in favor of the draft resolution as a whole.

We are aware of the desire to move swiftly to the vote, so I shall conclude by recalling that there is, always has been, and always will be a need for the Council to ensure the maintenance of international peace and security, the supreme aspiration of the Charter. I have before me an ancient text which reminds us from the far-distant past that while there is a time for tension, for threats, and for the use of force, there is also a time for us to be a little more concerned with peace. The quotation is from Ecclesiastes; in the 1960s young Americans turned it into a song popular in the United States and around the world.

"To every thing there is a season, and a time to every purpose under heaven:

"A time to love, and a time to hate; a time of war, and a time of peace." [Eccl. 3:1 and 3:8]

Let us hope that some day, sooner rather than later, the Council can finally devote some time to efforts that will not lead to war, but that will give peace a chance.

The Preacher also said, "Wisdom is better than might, though the poor man's wisdom is despised, and his words are not heeded." [Eccl. 9:16]

8

'We have been juggling words while the U.S. was announcing the dispatch of another 100,000 soldiers'

Resolution 674 (1990)

SECURITY COUNCIL, OCTOBER 29, 1990

The following resolution was adopted by a vote of 13-0-2, with Cuba and Yemen abstaining.

THE SECURITY COUNCIL,

RECALLING its resolutions 660 (1990), 661 (1990), 662 (1990), 664 (1990), 665 (1990), 666 (1990), 667 (1990), and 670 (1990),

STRESSING the urgent need for the immediate and unconditional withdrawal of all Iraqi forces from Kuwait, for the restoration of Kuwait's sovereignty, independence and territorial integrity and of the authority of its legitimate government,

CONDEMNING the actions by the Iraqi authorities and occupying forces to take third-state nationals hostage and to mistreat and oppress Kuwaiti and third-state nationals, and the other actions reported to the Council such as the destruction of Kuwaiti demographic records, forced departure of Kuwaitis and relocation of population in Kuwait and the unlawful destruction and seizure of public and private property in Kuwait including hospital supplies and equipment, in violation of the decisions of this Council, the Charter of the United Nations, the Fourth Geneva Convention, the Vienna Conventions on Diplomatic and Consular Relations and international law,

EXPRESSING grave alarm over the situation of nationals of third states in Kuwait and Iraq, including the personnel of the diplomatic and consular missions of such states,

REAFFIRMING that the Fourth Geneva Convention applies to Kuwait and that as a high contracting party to the convention, Iraq is bound to comply fully with all its terms and in particular is liable under the convention in respect of the grave breaches committed by it, as are individuals who commit or order the commission of grave breaches,

RECALLING the efforts of the secretary-general concerning the safety and well-being of third-state nationals in Iraq and Kuwait,

DEEPLY CONCERNED at the economic cost, and at the loss and suffering caused to individuals in Kuwait and Iraq as a result of the invasion and occupation of Kuwait by Iraq,

ACTING under Chapter 7 of the United Nations Charter,

REAFFIRMING the goal of the international community of maintaining international peace and security by seeking to resolve international disputes and conflicts through peaceful means,

RECALLING ALSO the important role that the United Nations and its secretary-general have played in the peaceful solution of disputes and conflicts in conformity with the provisions of the United Nations Charter,

ALARMED by the dangers of the present crisis caused by the Iraqi invasion and occupation of Kuwait, directly threatening international peace and security, and seeking to avoid any further worsening of the situation,

CALLING UPON Iraq to comply with the relevant resolutions of the Security Council, in particular resolutions 660 (1990), 662 (1990), and 664 (1990),

REAFFIRMING its determination to insure compliance by Iraq with the Security Council resolutions by maximum use of political and diplomatic means:

A

1. DEMANDS that the Iraqi authorities and occupying forces immediately cease and desist from taking third-state nationals hostage, mistreating and oppressing Kuwaiti and third-state nationals, and from any other actions such as those reported to the Council and described above, violating the decisions of this Council, the Charter of the United Nations, the Fourth Geneva Convention, the Vienna Conventions on Diplomatic and Consular Relations, and international law;

2. INVITES states to collate substantiated information in their possession or submitted to them on the grave breaches by Iraq as per paragraph 1 above and to make this information available to the Council;

3. REAFFIRMS its demand that Iraq immediately fulfill its obligations to third-state nationals in Kuwait and Iraq, including the personnel of diplomatic and consular missions, under the Charter, the Fourth Geneva Convention, the Vienna Conventions on Diplomatic and Consular Relations, general principles of international law, and the relevant resolutions of the Council;

4. REAFFIRMS FURTHER its demand that Iraq permit and facilitate the immediate departure from Kuwait and Iraq of those

third-state nationals, including diplomatic and consular personnel, who wish to leave;

5. DEMANDS that Iraq insure the immediate access to food, water, and basic services necessary to the protection and well-being of Kuwaiti nationals and of nationals of third states in Kuwait and Iraq, including the personnel of diplomatic and consular missions in Kuwait;

6. REAFFIRMS its demand that Iraq immediately protect the safety and well-being of diplomatic and consular personnel and premises in Kuwait and in Iraq, take no action to hinder these diplomatic and consular missions in the performance of their functions, including access to their nationals and the protection of their person and interests, and rescind its orders for the closure of diplomatic and consular missions in Kuwait and the withdrawal of the immunity of their personnel;

7. REQUESTS the secretary-general, in the context of the continued exercise of his good offices concerning the safety and well-being of third-state nationals in Iraq and Kuwait, to seek to achieve the objectives of paragraphs 4, 5, and 6 and in particular the provision of food, water, and basic services to Kuwaiti nationals and to the diplomatic and consular missions in Kuwait and the evacuation of third-state nationals;

8. REMINDS Iraq that under international law it is liable for any loss, damage, or injury arising in regard to Kuwait and third states, and their nationals and corporations, as a result of the invasion and illegal occupation of Kuwait by Iraq;

9. INVITES states to collect relevant information regarding their claims, and those of their nationals and corporations, for restitution or financial compensation by Iraq with a view to such arrangements as may be established in accordance with international law;

10. REQUIRES that Iraq comply with the provisions of the present resolution and its previous resolutions, failing which the Security Council will need to take further measures under the Charter;

11. DECIDES to remain actively and permanently seized of the matter until Kuwait has regained its independence and peace has been restored in conformity with the relevant resolutions of the Security Council;

B

12. REPOSES its trust in the secretary-general to make available his good offices and, as he considers appropriate, to pursue them and undertake diplomatic efforts in order to reach a peaceful solution to the crisis caused by the Iraqi invasion and occupation of Kuwait on the basis of Security Council resolutions 660 (1990), 662 (1990), and 664 (1990), and calls on all states, both those in the region and others, to pursue on this basis their efforts to this end, in conformity with the Charter, in order to improve the situation and restore peace, security, and stability;

13. REQUESTS the secretary-general to report to the Security Council on the results of his good offices and diplomatic efforts.

'It is our duty to work to prevent this war'

RICARDO ALARCON, OCTOBER 29, 1990

The following remarks were made during the discussion of Security Council Resolution 674 (1990).

In recent days, the members of the Security Council have been engrossed in lengthy disquisitions on substance and on form. We have gone around in circles in an endless squabble over preambles, operative parts, and their various possible combinations. We have done much juggling with letters, numbers, and asterisks.

Meanwhile, during these very days, the government of the United States was announcing the dispatch of another 100,000 soldiers to the region we are discussing. At the same time the leaders of the U.S. administration and Congress were openly discussing how to begin the military attack, whether or not there would be a declaration of war, whether authorization would be requested from the Senate or whether that body would merely be consulted, and whether this Council would be used for that stated purpose in some manner.

Some people may have been surprised that the Security Council was absent from that debate taking place elsewhere. They may have been surprised had they recalled the terms of paragraph 4 of Resolution 665 (1990), which this council adopted two months ago:

"Further requests the states concerned to coordinate their actions in pursuit of the above paragraphs of this resolution using, as appropriate, mechanisms of the Military Staff Committee, and, after consultation with the secretary-general, to submit reports to the Security Council and its committee established under Resolution 661 (1990) to facilitate the monitoring of the implementation of this resolution."

One might have imagined that this very substantial increase in military forces—which, it is claimed, is in keeping with the Council resolution I have just cited—had something to do with monitoring the implementation of that resolution. One might also have imagined that the Council's members—two months after the adoption of Resolution 665 (1990), when we are witnessing ongoing discussions on television as to how the war might begin, who would authorize it, and how the decision would be made—might have received at least the first of the reports they had sought when they adopted the resolution. The entire Council, legally speaking, had decided that such reports would be presented, since it was presumed that this body would constantly monitor the resolution's implementation.

No doubt we should be grateful to the distinguished representative of the United States for the courtesy and discretion he has maintained, in order to avoid diverting the attention of Council members from the important metaphysical disquisitions that took up so much of our time in recent days.

The outcome of those negotiations was the resolution the Council adopted a few moments ago. In this regard, my delegation would like to make a few comments.

To begin with, it seems obvious that Kuwait has the right to claim compensation for losses and damages caused as a result of the invasion and occupation of its territory. This Council has already formulated and repeated its view as to who is the aggressor and who is the victim. There was therefore no need for another resolution by this Council to affirm the inherent rights of the victim of aggression—in this case Kuwait.

But that is not really the intention behind the resolution just adopted. In the view of my delegation, the purpose is to delay a settlement of the conflict in the region and to make more difficult the mission of the secretary-general. More than once today we have heard about the circumstances of last Saturday and about the prudent decision we all made to wait a few days before submitting this text to a vote.[42] One would have to wonder whether there is any relationship between the vote on this resolution and certain efforts involving good offices and certain efforts for peace. One might also wonder how the Council interprets its own action in deciding today to adopt a resolution that, among other things, requests our own secretary-general to undertake similar efforts.

This text also seeks, in our opinion, to give the Security Council certain tasks that do not fall within its purview, and at the same time to prevent the Council from discharging certain obligations that it does have. First and foremost, it should be pointed out that Chapter 7 of the Charter—under which the resolution is being adopted—does not give the Security Council any authority whatsoever with respect to legal issues or issues that should be determined by courts of law. Neither that chapter nor any chapter of the Charter grants such functions to the Security Council.

Under the Charter, the Security Council does not have powers of a court to hand down decisions on liability or to determine compensation or restitution. The only reference in the Charter to such matters appears in Article 92, which clearly defines the International Court of Justice as the principal judicial organ of the United Nations. The only reference in the entire Charter to the issue of compensation or restitution is to be found in Article 36 of the Statute of the International Court of Justice.[43] In this regard, I hope that all the members of the Council recall that this statute is an integral part of the UN Charter itself.

In case there are any doubts about the functions and powers of the various organs created by the Charter, it should be said that the Charter does not confer upon the Council any authority to decide upon or even to discuss the functions and powers of the respective organs. These are powers clearly conferred upon the General Assembly, as is explicitly stated in Article 10 of the San Francisco Charter. Dealing with the powers of the General Assembly, the document states that the Assembly may discuss questions "relating to the powers and functions of any organs provided for in the present Charter."

In addition, one would have to ask what specific powers the Council is giving itself under the terms of operative paragraph 2

of Resolution 674 (1990), wherein it seeks to collect substantiated information of "grave breaches by Iraq as per its paragraph
1 above," and calls upon states to provide that information.
What will the Council do with that information? What powers
has it taken upon itself? Are we turning ourselves into a court of
law, despite the fact that the Charter tells us we are not the ones
who have this responsibility?

Paragraphs 8 and 9 of Resolution 674 (1990) contain references to international law. There is a contradiction here since,
as we understand it, the Charter and the Statute of the Court are
part of international law. It could be inferred from these paragraphs that we have some powers to hand down decisions about
liability and responsibility for compensation and restitution "as
a result of the invasion and illegal occupation of Kuwait by
Iraq."

The "result of the invasion and illegal occupation of Kuwait"
is a concept that can have many interpretations. Does it perhaps
mean that Iraq is judged to bear the responsibility and thus
must shoulder the cost of the military deployment being carried
out by some powers in the Gulf region? Does it mean that Iraq
bears exclusive responsibility for damages affecting third states
as a result of the crisis or of the decisions adopted by the
Council to deal with the crisis? Given the wording of the resolution, it could be interpreted as such. Does this mean then that
the Security Council is refusing to shoulder its responsibilities
under Article 50 of the Charter?

Might this be the reason why in the first paragraph of the
preamble to this text—which recalls a number of resolutions,
starting with Resolution 660 (1990), all of which refer to this
conflict—no mention is made of Resolution 669 (1990),[44] the
only resolution adopted thus far by the Council on the issue of
fulfilling its responsibilities under Article 50 of the Charter? Is
this a way of saying that we intend to formally enshrine the
inertia and insensitivity of this Council toward the many requests for assistance submitted to it by numerous states belonging to the United Nations, to help them deal with the adverse
impact stemming from the implementation of Resolution 661
(1990)?

If that is the case, we believe the Council is not only trying to
take upon itself powers it does not have; it is also indirectly
attempting to avoid the fulfillment of responsibilities it does
have, ones it should not fail to comply with.

Operative paragraph 12 of this resolution refers to the secretary-general of the United Nations. Above all it is quite striking how very different paragraph 12 reads from paragraph 7. When reference is made in paragraph 7 to the "safety and well-being of third-state nationals in Iraq and Kuwait," the Council does not hesitate to refer to "the continued exercise of his good offices," referring to the secretary-general. When it comes to this very important but limited aspect of the issue, we seem to be willing to speak of the continued exercise of the good offices of the secretary-general. But when it comes to examining the possibility of a peaceful solution of the crisis, when it comes to facing the key issue, the more substantive issue, we use language that is, to say the least, strange.

First we say the Council "reposes its trust in the secretary-general." Clearly all of us have reposed our trust in him—when we elected him, when we reelected him, and throughout his term of office. But now we don't even say he should exercise his good offices, much less continue what he has been doing; rather that he should make them available. This would appear to indicate the Council's reluctance to support and promote the efforts that the secretary-general himself has been making, even before the Council explicitly asked him to do so.

During the past few months, however, an effort has been made to get this Council to support clearly and without hesitation the possibility of diplomatic efforts, efforts for peace, which we are convinced the secretary-general can carry out.

It is curious that we have had to confront such difficulties when we recall another Security Council resolution mentioned in the first paragraph of the preamble here: Resolution 670 (1990). In one of the preambular paragraphs of Resolution 670 (1990) it says the following:

"Welcoming the secretary-general's use of his good offices to advance a peaceful solution based on the relevant Security Council resolutions and noting with appreciation his continuing efforts to this end."

After such a great effort to achieve the wording of operative paragraph 12 of today's resolution, one would have to wonder whether the Security Council really welcomes the efforts of the secretary-general in this crisis. Have we really expressed our gratitude for these continuing efforts that we noted barely a month ago, on September 25?

My delegation would like to reiterate its full confidence in the secretary-general, not only because of his sensitivity and awareness as an eminent diplomat, a worthy citizen of the world, a man of responsibility, who has already done and we are certain is ready to continue doing everything he can to ensure that peace will prevail, and to achieve implementation of this Council's resolutions in a peaceful manner.

We regret that the Security Council has not been able to express more clearly and less hesitantly this recognition and support. Yet we continue to place our confidence in him, in his ability and will, for among other things he has to face not only the great complexities of the issues we are discussing, but also the peculiar manner in which this body has been dealing with them.

In our view, despite the fact that this resolution contains—albeit in a limited manner—this positive ingredient regarding the efforts of the secretary-general, it is, as a whole, one more step toward war.

In this specific case, there might even be attempts to manipulate peace efforts. This has in fact occurred during the long period of negotiations over what were originally two separate texts.

It is also a step along a course we believe to be unacceptable: giving this body functions that are outside its purview, and which it has no right whatsoever to assume. This is true even if at a given moment temporary majorities may make it possible to garner the necessary votes to reinterpret the Charter and have this Council assume responsibilities not given it by the Charter.

In addition, we believe that from a political and moral standpoint, the Security Council—and some of the resolution's co-sponsors in particular—is not the best qualified to take up issues such as those dealt with in Resolution 674 (1990).

At one time, ports in Nicaragua were mined and a dirty war was launched against that country. This member state of the Organization went to the highest court of the United Nations, our court, the International Court of Justice. And that court attributed liability and handed down decisions that were never respected by the main proponent of this resolution.[45]

For twenty-three years the territories of Palestine have been occupied by a foreign power. Very soon, we hope, we shall once again be considering a report on the situation prevailing in that occupied country, to see what we can do to protect the lives of its inhabitants. I wonder whether at that time someone will recall the need for us to turn ourselves into a court. Or will we once again adopt the traditional phlegmatic attitude of this Council when it comes to dealing with the occupation of Palestine? Does an occupation and its tragic consequences for the victims cease to be a violation of the law because they have been going on for twenty-three years? Is it permissible to violate international law? Is it normal to take no action with respect to that aggression's tragic effects upon its victims simply because the aggressor has been able to flout the will of the international community for twenty-three years?

We still do not know how many died as a result of the U.S. invasion of Panama, or what the impact of that aggression was and still is for many citizens of that country. Can we be confident that at some point this Council will state its views on that insidious military attack or concern itself with the consequences, past and present, of this event for the population of that country?

We have heard statements—and we believe them to be legitimate—regarding the concern that everyone should feel about the violations that the occupier may be committing against the

U.S. troops arresting Panamanian citizens during December 1989 invasion. (Photo: AP/Wide World)

Kuwaiti population: violations of their individual rights, their human rights, their property rights, their right to live in peace and tranquility in their own country. It seems to us that this concern is legitimate. But it is and must be legitimate in all cases where international law is violated and aggression is committed against peoples.

Many thousands of Angolan children are suffering the irreparable consequences of the antipersonnel mines laid in that country by armed bands financed, organized, and equipped by the United States. It is not difficult to get the facts; if the Security Council wishes to collect the information, it exists and is well known. The figures are shocking, just as shocking as are the terrible consequences of this war for future Angolan generations. And this is a war imposed from the outside with the support and encouragement of a major power, a permanent member of this body.

The references would be endless if we were to cite all the examples of this Council's inconsistency.

Due to the tendency to repeat certain adjectives, the Security Council is frequently called an "august body." The term *august* seems to us to be an appropriate one for the Council, because more than once we have noted a certain imperious air in the manner with which some try to use and handle this body. We believe the Council quite justly repudiates the aggression against Kuwait and justly demands the immediate and unconditional withdrawal of the troops occupying that country. It proclaims its support for the independence, sovereignty, and territorial integrity of Kuwait, and has rightly spoken out against the claims of its annexation and against certain unlawful acts committed by Iraq against diplomatic missions and foreigners residing in Kuwait and Iraq.

However, we believe that while adhering to its just position with regard to these principles, the Council cannot and must not act as if it is permissible to accept the imposition of criteria and strategies devised solely for the benefit of certain major powers. It seems to us that to the extent that we do this, we move further and further away from our fundamental duty, which is to preserve peace. At the same time we come closer—inadvertently and without even realizing it, without anyone telling us, and despite all the resolutions of this body—to a war. This is a war we must not allow, much less foster, and it is our duty to work to prevent it.

'We had the honor of being the only country to vote 'No'!

'We have made many efforts for a political, not military, solution to the conflict'

FIDEL CASTRO, SEPTEMBER 28, 1990

The following is an excerpt from the speech delivered by Fidel Castro in Havana at the main ceremony celebrating the thirtieth anniversary of the Committees for the Defense of the Revolution.

In recent days we have been more than a little concerned about the fate of dozens and dozens of Third World countries. You will have noted the conduct of our representative on the United Nations Security Council around the crisis in the Arab-Persian Gulf. We have the privilege of being able to act there in a completely selfless manner, in a completely dignified manner, and with a spirit of complete fairness. We have made extraordinary efforts to achieve peace. We have sought to find a solution to the problem without war, a solution that is just.

We did not hesitate to reject and condemn the occupation and annexation of Kuwait. We did so as a matter of principle and on the basis of norms of international law that we believe should hold sway in our world. We therefore did not hesitate to support resolutions condemning those actions that, in our judgment, violated international law.

But at the same time, we have energetically opposed everything we consider unjust. And one of the most unjust things is the attempt to force an entire people to surrender through hunger. This is what the embargo amounts to.

We first of all energetically fought to exclude food and medicine from the embargo. For if one can condemn the practice of taking hostages and turning innocent persons into hostages—a practice we oppose and will always oppose—it is even more cruel to try to starve to death millions of women, elderly people, and children to attain a given objective. And this embargo does not affect the military forces primarily. Rather it causes suffering to the civilian population, and among them to millions of women, elderly people, and children.

This is a detestable practice. Yet this is what the United States has sought to do and has done, in opposition to Cuba's efforts to clearly define the embargo and to exclude from it food and medicine.

The United States has been devising procedures that make it practically impossible to send food and medicine. You can thus see how on the one hand they talk of human rights and they talk of certain principles, while on the other hand they apply incredibly cruel and detestable methods.

This we have categorically opposed, just as we did not vote in favor of the embargo, because we knew what was coming next. Hardly had the resolution on the embargo been approved in the UN, when the United States unilaterally decided to establish a naval blockade on its own, without United Nations authorization.

But then something occurred that was truly shameful: the Security Council passed a resolution giving its blessing to the unilateral blockade by the United States, a resolution we opposed. I believe that was a shameful day, a dishonorable day for the Security Council—the day that body gave its blessing to unilateral military action by the United States. At that moment it became clear that the United States was running the show in the Security Council.

Now they have approved an air embargo. Cuba voted against it, the only country to do so! We had the honor and glory of being the only country to vote "No"! [*Prolonged applause*] History will record the honor, the dignity, and the courage with which Cuba acted during that moment of such importance to the life of humanity. It was necessary to take a firm position and we did not abstain—we voted "No"! And we will vote against everything we do not agree with, even if we are the only ones. [*Applause*]

While several of the resolutions approved in the Security Council lead to war, we have fought for peace in the Security Council. And not only there, but everywhere, because we have made many silent, quiet efforts in the search for a political, not military, solution to the conflict. We have actively made use of our relations with many countries, trying to attain this objective.

A political solution, in our opinion, necessarily includes an end to the occupation of Kuwait and the reestablishment of that country's sovereignty. Of this we have no doubt whatsoever. Our line is principled, firm, and clear.

We believe there should be guarantees for all the countries of the region. And we believe that if the United Nations is able to achieve a political solution, it could also work out formulas to provide guarantees to all the countries of the region. This would include both the withdrawal of Iraqi troops to their border and their territory, and the withdrawal of U.S. and NATO troops from the Arab-Persian Gulf.

Failure to attain a political solution would be a defeat for humanity, and we have concentrated our efforts on achieving such a political solution. We have worked for this and continue to do so, although we are aware that less and less time remains.

We do this not only because it flows from the political principles of our people and our revolution, and not only to fulfill international obligations. We do this because it genuinely pains us very much to see a world catastrophe approaching, and not able to be halted. And here we are not dealing with a catastrophe of nuclear weapons, no—although no one knows what will happen there. No one can say for sure whether of not chemical weapons and nuclear weapons will be used.

But such a war will not only cost many lives on the battlefield there. Such a war would also be a catastrophe for the world economy, especially for the economies of the developing countries, of the non-oil-producing Third World countries, which are

Demonstration in Seattle, September 1990, one of many protests across the United States opposing Washington's war moves in the Middle East. (Photo: Margarita Kurtz/Militant)

the vast majority. Just as some countries will be swimming in money, others will be swimming in misery, sacrifice, and suffering of every type. For every life lost on the battlefields of the Arab-Persian Gulf, a thousand persons will die of hunger in the Third World. Such a fate would be unavoidable.

The outbreak of a conflict in the Arab-Persian Gulf—the military solution—would entail the risk of becoming a chemical war, and perhaps a war involving the use of tactical nuclear weapons. In addition, there would be incalculable destruction not only of lives but of energy resources, which are becoming more and more each day the Achilles' heel of the world economy and the economies of Third World countries.

If, on top of the enormous debt of over $1 trillion that these countries owe, one now adds oil priced at $60 or $70 a barrel, you can imagine the catastrophe. This has been an additional motivation for us to multiply our efforts for peace, in the Security Council and everywhere else.

It can be said that the United States and the Western powers have been focusing their efforts on war, a war that will even produce quite negative consequences for the economies of the developed countries and for the economy of the United States itself. I'm sure that if they were capable of thinking calmly, they would convince themselves that war is the worst solution for resolving this conflict; that the conflict can and should be resolved politically. Several of the resolutions adopted by the Security Council, rather than facilitating the road to a political solution, have moved further away from it and made it more complicated.

At this moment as well, our country is waging a great struggle in the UN. We have not been doing so thinking of our own interests—although our interests are wrapped up in this problem—but thinking of the interests of the entire world, and primarily the interests of the peoples of the Third World.

We will continue waging this honorable and at times solitary battle. We will not give up our principles, we will not vacillate, and we will not retreat!

NOTES

1. The membership of the UN Security Council at the time of the Iraqi government's invasion of Kuwait consisted of the five permanent members with veto power—Britain, China, France, the Soviet Union, and the United States—and ten nonpermanent members, each elected for two years—Canada, Colombia, Cuba, Ethiopia, Finland, the Ivory Coast, Malaysia, Romania, Yemen, and Zaire.

2. Article 39 of the UN Charter provides that "the Security Council shall determine the existence of any threat to the peace" and "decide what measures shall be taken." Article 40 states that these steps may include "provisional measures" decided "without prejudice to the rights, claims, or position of the parties concerned."

3. The Arab League is an association of twenty governments and the Palestine Liberation Organization. It was founded in 1945 to promote unity and common action among governments of countries with predominantly Arab populations.

4. The Movement of Nonaligned Countries, founded in 1961, encompasses more than one hundred governments and national liberation movements in the colonial and semicolonial world.

5. Article 51 of the UN Charter states, "Nothing in the present Charter shall impair the inherent right of individual or collective self-defense, if an armed attack occurs against a member of the United Nations, until the Security Council has taken measures necessary to maintain international peace and security."

6. Chapter 7 of the UN Charter, which includes articles 39 to 51, is entitled, "Action with Respect to Threats to the Peace, Breaches of the Peace, and Acts of Aggression."

7. The presidency of the Security Council rotates each month. In August it was held by Romania, whose ambassador to the United Nations is Aurel Manteanu.

8. On August 5, 1990, the day before Alarcón's remarks, Washington dispatched an airborne contingent of 255 marines to civil war-torn Monrovia, Liberia, declaring they would "remain as long as necessary to assure the security" of U.S. citizens.

9. Troops of the South African apartheid regime, with the backing of Washington, invaded Angola in 1975. Their attempt to overturn the government of the newly independent state was blocked, however, thanks to the assistance of Cuban volunteer troops. The South African government continued its war against Angola until 1988,

when its army was decisively defeated by Cuban, Angolan, and Namibian forces at Cuito Cuanavale.

10. Israeli troops have occupied southern Lebanon since an invasion mounted in March 1978, and have carried out many bloody military operations throughout Lebanese territory. Shortly after the 1978 invasion, a small UN observer mission was stationed in southern Lebanon.

11. U.S. troops invaded Panama December 20, 1989, installing Guillermo Endara as the country's new president the same day. Endara was sworn in at Fort Clayton, a U.S. military base in the canal zone.

12. The four members of the Security Council whose representatives voted against the resolution on Panama were Britain, Canada, France, and the United States.

13. The message that follows was also sent to the governments of the Soviet Union, China, India, and Yugoslavia, to the Arab League and the Organization of African Unity, and to members of the UN General Assembly.

14. Article 42 of the UN Charter provides that when other measures prove inadequate, the Security Council may utilize armed force to "maintain or restore international peace and security."

15. The *intifada* is the uprising sustained since December 1987 by Palestinians and their supporters against Israeli rule of the occupied territories.

16. In October 1983, the U.S. government invaded and occupied Grenada and set about to forcibly reverse the gains of that country's 1979 revolution. Two weeks before the U.S. attack, the People's Revolutionary Government of Grenada, headed by Maurice Bishop, had been overthrown by a counterrevolutionary coup led by Deputy Prime Minister Bernard Coard.

17. On April 14, 1986, U.S. warplanes bombed Libyan population centers, targeting in particular the home of Libyan head of state Muammar Qaddafi. One of Qaddafi's children was killed in the raid.

18. In October 1962 the U.S. government blockaded Cuba and threatened it with nuclear annihilation if Soviet missiles installed there at Cuba's request to defend the island against U.S. attack were not removed. The Soviet government, without consulting the Cuban government, agreed to withdraw the missiles.

19. The document in question was prepared by the International Centre against Apartheid in London.

20. The following day, August 10, representatives of the Arab League met in Cairo. A resolution was passed, supported by delegates of twelve governments, to send troops to join those of the United States and its allies in Saudi Arabia and other Arab-Persian Gulf states. Other delegations voted no, abstained, or voted yes with reservations.

21. On August 17 an informal meeting of Security Council members, convened at Britain's request, considered the question of nationals of third countries within Iraq and Kuwait.

22. In 1942, following U.S. entry into World War II, 112,000 people of Japanese descent living on the West Coast were placed in concentration camps. The action was carried out by executive order, and those incarcerated, including those who were U.S. citizens, were denied the right to legal redress guaranteed them by the Constitution. Only in 1988 did the U.S. government by an act of Congress finally apologize for this brutal deed and offer token compensation to the surviving victims.

23. Following the invasion of Panama in December 1989, U.S. troops blockaded the Cuban Embassy, established a cordon around the Papal Nunciature, and raided the residence of the Nicaraguan ambassador.

24. Article 41 of the UN Charter empowers the Security Council, in seeking to secure compliance with its decisions, to decide on "measures not involving the use of armed force"—such as economic, transportation, and communications embargoes—and to call on UN members to enforce such measures.

25. The Military Staff Committee was established by the UN Charter to organize military enforcement of Security Council decisions. It is composed of the chiefs of staff of the five powers that hold permanent veto power in the Security Council. No UN forces have ever been placed under its command.

26. Article 43, paragraph 1, of the Charter provides that, at the call of the Security Council, all members of the United Nations will make available armed forces necessary to maintain "international peace and security."

Article 46 states that the Security Council, assisted by the Military Staff Committee, will control the use of armed force to implement its decisions.

Article 47, paragraph 1 outlines the functions of the Military Staff Committee.

According to Article 48, paragraph 1, the Security Council determines which members of the United Nations will take part in the enforcement of the Council's decisions.

At the start of the 1950-53 Korean War, the Security Council adopted resolutions calling on member countries to give military assistance to South Korea, and established a unified command whose commander was to be designated by the United States. The unified command was authorized to use the UN flag. Fifteen member nations sent armed contingents to join Washington's forces.

At the time the resolution was adopted in 1950, the Soviet Union was boycotting meetings of the Security Council to protest the refusal of the United Nations to seat the People's Republic of China. The Soviet Union and numerous other UN members have always denied the legitimacy of U.S. claims that the troops in Korea under U.S. command were UN forces.

28. The Fourth Geneva Convention, part of an international treaty concluded in 1949, concerns protection of civilian populations during war. One of its provisions forbids the taking of hostages.

29. The presidency of the Security Council for the month of September was held by the Soviet Union, whose ambassador to the United Nations is Yuliy Vorontsov.

30. The sanctions committee, headed by Marjatta Rasi of Finland and composed of all members of the Security Council, was established by Resolution 661 (1990) to oversee implementation of the trade embargo against Iraq.

31. Article 50 states, "If preventative or enforcement measures against any state are taken by the Security Council, any other state, whether a member of the United Nations or not, which finds itself confronted with special problems arising from the carrying out of those measures shall have the right to consult the Security Council with regard to a solution of those problems."

32. Starting September 1, several flights left Baghdad, the capital of Iraq, evacuating more than one thousand citizens of the United States, Japan, and several countries of Europe.

33. A special session of the UN General Assembly on apartheid, meeting December 13-14, 1989, unanimously adopted a declaration setting out guidelines for South Africa's transition to a nonracial democracy.

34. Security Council Resolution 418 (1977) established a mandatory arms embargo against South Africa. Resolution 421 (1977) set up a committee made up of all Council members to oversee implementation of the embargo. In 1963 the Security Council passed Resolution 181 calling for a "voluntary arms embargo" against South Africa.

35. Article 25 states, "The members of the United Nations agree to accept and carry out the decisions of the Security Council in accordance with the present Charter."

36. Article 48 states that "action required to carry out decisions of the Security Council . . . shall be taken by all the members of the United Nations, or by some of them as the Security Council may determine."

37. According to Article 103, the obligations of members of the United Nations under its Charter take precedence over obligations under any other international agreement.

38. UNIIMOG is the United Nations Iran-Iraq Military Observation Group, which is stationed at the border between Iran and Iraq.

39. This is a reference to the Convention on International Civil Aviation, signed in Chicago, December 7, 1944.

40. The September 25 session of the Security Council was presided over by Eduard Shevardnadze, foreign minister of the Soviet Union.

41. In August 1974 the Turkish government invaded Cyprus and partitioned the island. In 1983 it established a separate regime under its domination in the north.

42. On Saturday, October 27, the Security Council decided to postpone a vote on this resolution. The representative of the Soviet Union had requested the delay because an emissary of Soviet president Gorbachev was then in Baghdad to meet with Iraqi government authorities.

43. The International Court of Justice is also known as the World Court, located at The Hague, Netherlands. Article 92 of the Charter states, "The International Court of Justice shall be the principal judicial organ of the United Nations." Article 36 states, "The Security Council may . . . recommend appropriate procedures or methods of adjustment." These recomendations, "should as a general rule be referred by the parties to the International Court of Justice."

44. Resolution 669 (1990) was passed by the Security Council on September 24. It read:

"*The Security Council,*

"*Recalling* its Resolution 661 (1990) of 6 August 1990,

"*Recalling also* Article 50 of the Charter of the United Nations,

"*Conscious* of the fact that an increasing number of requests for assistance have been received under the provisions of Article 50 of the Charter of the United Nations,

"*Entrusts* the committee established under Resolution 661 (1990)

concerning the situation between Iraq and Kuwait with the task of examining requests for assistance under the provisions of Article 50 of the Charter of the United Nations and making recommendations to the president of the Security Council for appropriate action."

45. In February 1984 the U.S. government began mining Nicaraguan ports. The Nicaraguan government protested this and placed its case before the International Court of Justice. In May 1984 the court ruled that the United States "should immediately cease and refrain from any action restricting, blocking or endangering access to or from Nicaraguan ports, and, in particular, the laying of mines." Washington announced it would not accept the court's jurisdiction in the matter.

In June 1986 the court ruled that the U.S. was "under an obligation to make reparations" to Nicaragua—a decision that Washington rejected.

CHRONOLOGY

July 17-18, 1990—Iraqi president Saddam Hussein accuses Kuwait and the United Arab Emirates of flooding the international oil market and driving prices down, thus costing Iraq $14 billion in lost oil revenue. He also accuses Kuwait of stealing $2.4 billion in Iraqi oil from wells in the Rumaila oil field along the disputed border between the two countries.

Earlier Kuwait rejects Iraqi claims to the Kuwaiti islands of Bubiyan and Warbah at the head of the Arab-Persian Gulf; control of these islands would give Iraq easy access to the sea.

July 25—U.S. ambassador to Iraq April Glaspie meets with Iraqi president Hussein and explains, "We have no opinion on the Arab-Arab conflicts, like your border disagreement with Kuwait. . . . If we are unable to find a solution, then it will be natural that Iraq will not accept death."

August 1—After one session, Iraq breaks off talks with Kuwait in Jidda, Saudi Arabia, on oil extraction levels and the border dispute.

August 2—Iraqi troops invade Kuwait and occupy the capital, Kuwait city. Kuwait's emir, Sheik Jaber al-Ahmed al-Sabah, flees to Saudi Arabia and establishes a government in exile. The Provisional Free Government of Kuwait announces over Iraqi radio that it is in full control.

U.S. president George Bush signs executive orders banning U.S. trade with Iraq, except for humanitarian aid such as medical supplies, and freezing $30 billion in Iraqi and Kuwaiti assets. The U.S. House of Representatives follows suit in a 416-0 vote imposing sanctions on Iraq.

Meeting in the United States, Bush and British prime minister Margaret Thatcher call for economic sanctions against Iraq.

Britain and France freeze Kuwaiti assets. The twelve-member European Community unanimously condemns the Iraqi invasion. The Soviet Union suspends arms sales to Iraq.

U.S. officials order a battle group of seven warships led by the aircraft carrier USS *Independence* to sail for the Arab-Persian Gulf from the Indian Ocean and shift the aircraft carrier USS *Eisenhower* and its twelve-ship battle group to the eastern Mediterranean Sea.

The fifteen-member UN Security Council, in a 14-0-1 vote,

passes **Resolution 660** condemning the Iraqi invasion of Kuwait and calling on Iraq to withdraw unconditionally. Yemen's representative abstains.

Cuban president Fidel Castro sends a letter to the Movement of Nonaligned Countries urging diplomatic efforts to find a peaceful solution and warning of the danger of U.S. intervention.

U.S. officials advise Israel against playing any public role in the unfolding situation. Israeli defense minister Moshe Arens calls for sanctions against Iraq.

Britain announces it is sending two frigates to the Gulf to join the destroyer HMS *York* and three other warships already there.

August 3—Representatives of the twenty-one-member Arab League meet in Cairo, Egypt. Fourteen delegations vote to demand immediate withdrawal of Iraqi troops.

U.S. secretary of state James Baker and Soviet foreign minister Eduard Shevardnadze issue a joint statement in Moscow calling for a worldwide end to arms shipments to Iraq.

Japan, West Germany, Belgium, Italy, and the Netherlands freeze Iraqi and Kuwaiti assets.

Despite near-record supplies worldwide, oil prices start to spiral upward. From $20.40 per barrel days before the invasion of Kuwait, they nearly double over the next six weeks. For every $1-per-barrel increase, $21 billion is extracted from the pockets of working people worldwide.

August 4—The European Community imposes economic sanctions on Iraq, including a ban on oil imports.

Baghdad television announces the composition of the new Kuwaiti government: nine men identified as Kuwaiti military officers.

August 5—Bush sends Defense Secretary Richard Cheney to Saudi Arabia to meet with King Fahd, who agrees, for the first time ever, to allow U.S. troops to be based in Saudi Arabia.

A contingent of 255 U.S. marines lands in Monrovia, Liberia, ostensibly to protect U.S. citizens in the midst of the civil war there.

Japan imposes economic sanctions on Iraq, including a ban on oil imports. China suspends arms sales to Iraq.

August 6—The aircraft carrier USS *Saratoga*—accompanied by its battle group that includes 2,100 marines, the battleship USS *Wisconsin,* guided-missile cruisers, and attack submarines— leaves Norfolk, Virginia, for the eastern Mediterranean to join the *Eisenhower.* The ships are carrying F-14 fighters, F-18 attack jets, and Tomahawk cruise missiles.

U.S. and British officials say they are prepared to organize a naval blockade of Iraq to enforce UN economic sanctions. Britain and France send more naval forces to the region.

The Security Council passes **Resolution 661,** 13-0-2, imposing an economic embargo on Iraq, the third country to be subject to such action in the UN's history. Humanitarian food aid and medicine are exempted. Cuba denounces U.S. war moves. Cuba and Yemen abstain. Less stringent embargoes were voted against Southern Rhodesia in 1967 and South Africa in 1963 and 1977.

August 7—Operation Desert Shield begins with thousands of U.S. paratroopers, an armored brigade, and jet fighters ordered to Saudi Arabia. Lightly equipped rapid deployment forces from the 82d Airborne and other units begin arriving the same day in what quickly becomes the largest U.S. military mobilization since the Vietnam War and the largest airlift since World War II. A brigade from the 24th Mechanized Infantry Division and units from the 101st Airborne equipped with helicopters are also to be sent. Egypt permits transit through the Suez Canal, as the *Eisenhower* battle group is ordered to the Arabian Sea.

Castro sends a letter to Arab heads of state warning of the dangers of U.S. intervention.

Turkish president Turgut Özal says Turkey will enforce sanctions and stop ships from loading Iraqi crude oil, in effect shutting down two Iraqi pipelines in Turkish territory.

August 8—The makeup of the nine-member Provisional Free Government of Kuwait is disclosed. All are Iraqi army officers.

The government of Iraq announces the annexation of Kuwait.

U.S. officials estimate that the size of U.S. ground forces will be 50,000 within a month.

August 9—The Security Council passes **Resolution 662,** 15 to 0, rejecting Iraq's annexation of Kuwait.

Turkey promises greater U.S. access to NATO air bases on its territory.

Some fifty U.S. and allied warships are now in the region.

U.S. officials appeal for ground troops to be sent by allies to join U.S. troops in Saudi Arabia.

August 10—Representatives of twelve members of the twenty-one-member Arab League, meeting in Cairo, vote to send troops to Saudi Arabia to join U.S.-led forces arrayed against Iraq.

Canada and Australia agree to send three warships each to the Gulf.

The Pentagon charters commercial airliners, including from strike-bound Eastern Airlines, to ferry troops and cargo.

The Bush administration announces that U.S., British, and French warships stationed near ports in the Gulf region will stop shipments of oil from Iraq.

U.S. deployment plans for air force units include sending 3 squadrons of F-16 fighters, nearly 100 A-10 antitank planes, 24 F-117A Stealth fighters, 12 AC-130 gunships, 18 F-111 bombers, 24 B-52G bombers, and a large number of C-130 transport planes.

Pentagon officials double the estimate of U.S. ground forces to be deployed to 100,000.

August 11—Egyptian paratroopers and commandos and Moroccan troops begin landing in Saudi Arabia.

Syria announces it will send 4,000 ground troops to join the U.S.-led forces.

August 12—U.S. officials report that U.S. naval forces are being given orders to enforce the embargo against Iraq, including against vessels carrying food. U.S. ground forces in Saudi Arabia number 5,000. During peak times one U.S. transport plane lands every ten minutes in Saudi Arabia.

France sends the aircraft carrier *Clemenceau* to the Gulf, with 600 paratroopers and 140 infantrymen aboard.

Tens of thousands in Jordan, the West Bank and Gaza Strip, Libya, Mauritania, Sudan, and Yemen protest U.S. moves. Antigovernment demonstrations are reported in Syria.

August 13—Britain declares its naval forces in the Gulf are prepared to enforce the embargo.

Iraq announces that foreign citizens will not be allowed to leave Iraq and Kuwait.

August 15—Another aircraft carrier, the USS *John F. Kennedy,* and its battle group depart for the Mediterranean.

Iraq offers Iran a permanent settlement, on terms highly

favorable to Iran, of the 1980-88 Gulf war launched by the Saddam Hussein regime's invasion of Iranian territory. Agreement is rapidly concluded.

August 16—UN secretary-general Javier Pérez de Cuéllar says unilateral U.S. action to enforce the embargo will violate the UN Charter.

A U.S. naval blockade of all shipping to and from Iraq begins.

Some 50,000 protest at the U.S. embassy in San'a, Yemen, calling for the immediate withdrawal of U.S. forces.

August 17—The Pentagon announces the first-ever activation of a 1951 emergency program, known as the Civil Reserve Air Fleet, to aid the military airlift by commandeering aircraft from civilian airline companies.

August 18—U.S. warships fire warning shots at Iraqi oil tankers.

The Security Council passes **Resolution 664,** 15 to 0, calling on Iraq to permit the departure of foreign citizens from Iraq and Kuwait.

August 21—Belgium, Italy, the Netherlands, and Spain announce they will send warships to the Gulf region. West Germany sends minesweepers to the eastern Mediterranean to fill in for other states' warships deployed to the Gulf.

August 22—The Bush administration begins calling up military reservists for noncombat active duty in the Gulf region. This is the first time since the January 1968 Tet Offensive during the Vietnam War that reservists have been called to active duty.

August 24—Iraqi troops surround foreign embassies in Kuwait city after they refuse Iraq's order to close and move to Baghdad. Water and electricity are shut off.

August 25—The Security Council passes **Resolution 665,** 13-0-2, authorizing member states to use "such measures . . . as may be necessary" against Iraq to enforce a trade embargo. Cuba denounces the action—the first in UN history where force is authorized to impose economic sanctions adopted by the United Nations. Cuba and Yemen abstain.

August 26—About 45,000 U.S. troops are now in Saudi Arabia.

Some 50,000 Syrian troops are sent to suppress large antigovernment protests in towns near the Syrian-Iraqi border.

Shevardnadze tells the press that the USSR will not object to other nations using military force to blockade Iraq.

August 29—Thirteen U.S. GIs die when their supply plane crashes in West Germany en route to the region.

August 30–September 1—Foreign ministers of thirteen of the twenty-one Arab League member states meet in Cairo. Algeria, Iraq, Jordan, Mauritania, the Palestine Liberation Organization, Sudan, Tunisia, and Yemen boycott the meeting.

UN-authorized U.S.- and British-chartered Iraqi Airways flights begin evacuating U.S., British, and other citizens from Iraq and Kuwait. Most are women and children. Flights continue for three weeks and then off and on into November.

Early September—India asks UN permission to send a boatload of food to Kuwait for tens of thousands of Indian citizens facing a severe food shortage. Tens of thousands more Sri Lankans, Filipinos, Vietnamese, and citizens of other nations face similar suffering.

September 4—Senegalese president Abdou Diouf announces he will send 500 troops to join the forces being arrayed against Iraq.

Turkish president Özal obtains special parliamentary approval to allow Turkey's NATO bases to receive foreign forces and be used for military operations against Iraq.

September 5—Britain and France stop arms sales to Jordan.

September 6—Refugees from Kuwait and Iraq who have passed through Jordan now surpass 600,000 in number, while 100,000 remain stranded there under desperate conditions. Most are Indian, Pakistani, Bangladeshi, Thai, or Filipino.

September 7—Britain drops its long-standing veto of European Community aid to Syria.

The Soviet Union announces the resumption of diplomatic relations with Saudi Arabia.

Niger announces the decision to send troops to Saudi Arabia.

September 9—Bush and Soviet president Mikhail Gorbachev meet in Helsinki, Finland.

September 10—Iraq and Iran restore diplomatic relations. Reports continue of trade in food, oil, and other commodities between the two countries.

September 12—Iranian leader Ayatollah Ali Khamenei denounces the U.S. buildup in the Gulf.

September 13—U.S. naval forces are now boarding three to four ships a day, mainly in the Red Sea, to check cargoes and destinations. U.S. Coast Guard officers assist the navy.

The Security Council passes **Resolution 666,** 13 to 2, restricting the shipment of food supplies to Iraq, with Cuba and Yemen voting against. A counterresolution by Cuba, affirming that access to food and adequate medical care are basic human rights, is defeated by a vote of 3 to 5 with 7 abstentions.

September 14—U.S. and Australian warships fire warning shots and forcibly board an Iraqi tanker.

Iraqi troops raid several diplomatic missions and residences in Kuwait city.

Britain announces it is sending the 7th Armoured Regiment with 8,000 troops and 120 Challenger tanks to Saudi Arabia. Canada says a squadron of CF-18 fighters will be deployed. Another frigate and eight Tornado aircraft will be sent by Italy.

The Pentagon approves more than $20 billion in arms sales to Saudi Arabia.

Mid-September—Tens of thousands of Yemenis working in Saudi Arabia begin leaving after their work permits are revoked in retaliation for Yemen's refusal to join the imperialist-led coalition against Iraq. An estimated two million Yemenis live in Saudi Arabia.

Saudi Arabia cuts off oil shipments to Jordan, whose vital port at Aqaba is nearly shut down by the embargo.

September 16—The Security Council passes **Resolution 667,** 15 to 0, protesting Iraqi violations of diplomatic immunity of foreign embassies and personnel in Kuwait.

West German chancellor Helmut Kohl calls for amending that state's 1949 constitution, which bars German military action outside of the NATO framework, and proposes sending German troops to the Gulf as soon as possible after the new, all-German parliament is elected.

France sends 4,000 more men, tanks, helicopters, and fighter planes to the Gulf following the ransacking of its Kuwait city diplomatic mission. French military strength reaches 13,000 troops and 14 warships in the region.

September 17—European Community governments decide to expel most Iraqi diplomats from their respective countries.

Egyptian troop strength in region is reported at 5,000.

The imminent departure for the Gulf of 500 Senegalese troops is announced.

September 21—Turkey's troop buildup, backed by tanks and warplanes, reaches 95,000 on the Turkish-Iraqi border.

Some 1,000 in Kaduna, northern Nigeria, protest war moves in front of the U.S. consulate.

September 24—Addressing the UN General Assembly, French president François Mitterrand calls on Iraq to "affirm its intention to withdraw from Kuwait and free the hostages," saying this would open the road to a negotiated solution.

Iranian foreign minister Ali Akbar Velayati, addressing the General Assembly, pledges Iran will not violate the trade embargo against Iraq.

The Security Council passes **Resolution 669,** 15 to 0, acknowledging the growing requests for assistance from member states suffering from the sanctions imposed against Iraq under Resolution 661.

September 25—U.S. troop strength exceeds 150,000, with more on the way.

Shevardnadze, in an address to the UN General Assembly, warns Iraq that "the United Nations has the power to suppress acts of aggression," and suggests it may be necessary for the Security Council to establish a "rapid response force" composed of units "designated by different countries, including all five permanent members of the Security Council."

The Security Council passes **Resolution 670,** 14 to 1, imposing an air embargo on Iraq. Cuba denounces this as an escalation of war preparations by Washington and its allies and votes against.

September 26—The number of U.S. military reservists called up for active duty in the Gulf as noncombatants reaches 21,000.

September 27—Japanese prime minister Toshiki Kaifu proposes sending lightly armed Japanese troops to the Gulf in a "noncombat" role to back up allied forces. If approved, the action would be the first overt use of Japanese troops outside of Japan since World War II. The proposal precipitates a storm of debate and protest.

The South Korean government pledges $150 million for maintenance of U.S. forces in Gulf.

Britain restores diplomatic relations with Iran broken off in March 1989 when Ayatollah Ruhollah Khomeini issued a death sentence against writer Salman Rushdie.

Oil prices rise to $39.54 per barrel.

Honduran president Rafael Callejas, at the White House, states his willingness to send a contingent to the Gulf.

September 30—The Soviet Union establishes diplomatic relations for the first time with South Korea and consular relations with Israel. Thatcher meets with Bush and proposes that the Security Council order Iraq to pay war reparations.

October 1—Bush addresses the UN General Assembly.

October 2—The U.S. aircraft carrier *Independence* and its battle group arrive in the Gulf—only the second time a U.S. aircraft carrier has ever done so—accompanied by four minesweepers. U.S. naval vessels in the Gulf, northern Arabian Sea, and Red Sea now total 54.

The French warship *Doudart de Lagrée* fires warning shots at a North Korean freighter, the *Sam Il Po,* near Djibouti in the Bab el Mandeb Strait. The freighter is boarded and then released, in the fifth such use of force since the naval blockade against Iraq began August 16.

October 3—Gorbachev sends Yevgeny Primakov, a Presidential Council member, to Jordan and Iraq. The Soviet magazine *Literaturnaya Gazeta* quotes Primakov: "I think we should proceed from the fact that [the Gulf crisis] offers a kind of laboratory, testing our efforts to create a new world order after the Cold War. Very much depends on Soviet-American solidarity, on parallel activity or joint political action, on mutual support."

Mitterrand begins a two-day visit to the Gulf, the first Western head of state to do so.

The total number of U.S. troops in the region now exceeds 170,000.

October 4—Japanese prime minister Kaifu visits Jordan and pledges $250 million in loans to offset the effects of the blockade of Iraq on Jordan's economy.

French Foreign Legion troops arrive in Kigali, Rwanda, to help put down a rebel insurgency. The first contingent of Belgian paratroopers joins them the next day.

October 8—Israeli police open fire on unarmed Palestinian protesters near Jerusalem's Al-Aqsa Mosque, killing 21 and wounding more than 100.

October 9—The Security Council begins debating its response to the Israeli massacre. Fearing its coalition against Iraq will be jeopardized, Washington sponsors a resolution condemning

Israel. Yemen sponsors a more strongly worded draft.

October 11—The U.S. 1st Cavalry Division, 3d Armored Cavalry Regiment, and units of the 2d Armored Division begin arriving in Saudi Arabia from Germany. The additional forces number 15,000 men with M-1 tanks and Bradley armored fighting vehicles, helping to transform the U.S. forces from lightly equipped rapid deployment forces capable of guarding oil fields and military installations into a substantial offensive force.

More than 130,000 Jordanian refugees who had been working in the Gulf region are now back in Jordan. Jordanian officials estimate they will need $300 million to provide them social services. Estimates of unemployment there range from 20 to 40 percent.

October 12—The Security Council passes U.S.-sponsored Resolution 672, 15 to 0, condemning the "acts of violence committed by the Israeli security forces" and calling on the secretary-general to send a fact-finding mission to Israel and to submit a report by the end of October.

World Bank officials let it be known that Iran's request for a $300 million loan, the first such request in eleven years, will probably be approved.

October 13—Syria consolidates effective military control over most of Lebanon by removing rightist general Michel Aoun from power, using aerial bombings at the presidential palace with prior Israeli and U.S. knowledge and acquiescence. The State Department says, "We hope this ends a sad chapter of Lebanon's history and that the Lebanese people can now move toward . . . a united, sovereign, and independent Lebanon.

October 14—The Israeli government vows not to cooperate with the UN fact-finding mission.

Mid-October—Jordan permits U.S. monitors to inspect truck cargo at the Jordanian-Iraqi border for compliance with the embargo against Iraq.

October 16—Japan's parliament begins debate on a plan to send Japanese troops to the Gulf in a noncombat role. Protests continue.

October 17—The Asian Development Bank announces that wages sent home by Asian workers in the Middle East could fall by $750 million in the second half of 1990 because of the Gulf crisis. The 3.5 million Asians working in the region send $10-12 billion home annually.

Economic losses for 1990-91 for Jordan, Egypt, and Turkey are estimated at $4 billion, $3 billion, and $5 billion respectively.

October 18—The U.S. Congress approves a complete ban on trade with Cuba by U.S. subsidiary companies based in other countries.

October 19—U.S. officials announce they are shipping 400 to 500 top-of-the-line M-1A1 tanks to Saudi Arabia from NATO storage in Germany, bringing the number of U.S. tanks there to more than 1,000. Delivery will take about seventeen days.

October 20—Thousands protest U.S. war moves in more than two dozen U.S. cities under the slogans "Bring the troops home now!" and "No war for oil company profits!" Speakers at the 10,000-strong New York and 5,000-strong San Francisco actions include several military reservists who are resisting deployment.

Thousands more take to the streets in some ten other countries.

Of the hundreds of millions of dollars pledged to Jordan to offset its economic crisis, only $4 million has reportedly been received.

October 25—Cheney, saying no "upper ceiling" had ever been set, announces U.S. plans to send up to 100,000 more troops to the region to join the 210,000 already deployed. In addition, close to 200,000 troops from U.S.-allied countries are now in the Gulf.

The Security Council passes a new resolution calling on the Israeli government to cooperate with the UN team established in Resolution 672, which is investigating the October 8 killings of Palestinians.

Yemeni president Ali Abdullah Saleh announces that more than 500,000 have returned to Yemen since mid-September after being forced to leave by the Saudi government. The expulsion will cost the Yemeni economy $350 million per month in lost remittances.

Canadian minister of external affairs Joseph Clark addresses the Canadian Parliament, saying his government is ready to join a military offensive against Iraq without waiting for UN approval. He later says, "War is possible. There will be thousands of casualties . . . and we should not rule out the possibility that young Canadian soldiers will not return to this country for celebration but will stay there for burial." Canadian troop strength reaches 1,700.

Britain agrees to put its 15,000-man force under U.S. command. France reportedly agrees to do the same with its 13,000 troops.

October 28—A decision to double the active-duty period of service for combat reservists from 180 days to 360 is quietly added to the 1991 U.S. military spending bill. There is no discussion or debate as Congress adjourns for the year. Included in the federal budget is $700 million more in U.S. weapons for Israel above the annual allocation of $5 billion.

October 29—The Security Council passes **Resolution 674,** 13-0-2, calling on Iraq to pay war reparations for its invasion and occupation of Kuwait to all parties involved. Cuba calls it "one more step toward war." Cuba and Yemen abstain.

October 30—Eleven U.S. servicemen are killed in two accidents, bringing the U.S. death toll to forty-three.

October 31—Bush warns he is prepared to air-drop supplies to the U.S. embassy in Kuwait city saying, "The American flag flies over the Kuwaiti embassy and our people inside are being starved by a brutal dictator."

November 1—Gen. Norman Schwarzkopf, commander of U.S. forces in the Gulf, says, "If we have to fight I am going to use everything that is available to me to inflict the maximum number of casualties on the enemy as possible." He promises to use "vastly superior firepower and technology" to "bring as much destruction on the Iraqi forces as rapidly as I possibly can."

November 2—Reservist Stephanie Atkinson is placed under arrest in Fort Knox, Kentucky, for refusing deployment to Saudi Arabia. She says, "I don't think the U.S. is participating in this for honest reasons. We're fighting for oil and our economy."

November 3—Saudi oil extraction reaches 8.2 million barrels a day, up from 5.4 million on August 2. This increase brings the world level back to what it was prior to the embargo on Iraqi and Kuwaiti output. Combined with the doubling of oil prices over this period, the Saudi regime is raking in more than $200 million a day extra, a fraction of which is being contributed to maintaining the U.S.-led military intervention.

Syrian officials voice support for offensive action against Iraq.

November 4—The Pentagon, citing the October 28 congressional decision doubling active-duty reserve service to 360 days, decides to call up thousands of combat reservists as part of the up-to-100,000 increase announced on October 25. More than 34,000 reservists have already been deployed in noncombat roles.

The first contingent of the 15,000-member Syrian 9th Armored Division, with the first of 270 tanks, lands in Saudi Arabia, which will bring its forces there to 19,000. The Syrians, along with other Arab troops, are deployed on the front lines.

Baker begins a week-long, eight-nation trip to obtain support for the direct use of military force against Iraq and agreement on how to coordinate offensive operations.

November 5—Baker, meeting with the Saudi foreign minister and King Fahd in Jidda, obtains agreement on giving the U.S. command structure a free hand in any offensive military action against Iraq.

November 6—Baker meets with Chinese foreign minister Qian Qichen in Cairo, seeking agreement that China will not block a UN resolution authorizing the direct use of force against Iraq.

UN-sponsored talks begin in Geneva, Switzerland, on the devastating effects of oil price increases due to the Gulf crisis.

November 7—Marjatta Rasi of Finland, who heads the UN sanctions committee that oversees the trade embargo against Iraq established by Resolution 661, acknowledges that no trade violations have ever been reported.

Thatcher tells the British House of Commons, "Either [President Saddam Hussein] gets out of Kuwait soon or we and our allies will remove him by force, and he will go down to defeat with all its consequences."

Egyptian president Hosni Mubarak, saying war is inevitable if Iraq does not withdraw from Kuwait soon, voices support for a UN resolution authorizing offensive action against Iraq and announces that another armored division with 400 tanks and 7,000 men will be in place in Saudi Arabia by the end of November. They will join the already fully deployed 15,000-man 3d Mechanized Division and other units.

African National Congress deputy president Nelson Mandela, in Paris, accuses the West of hypocrisy in its war moves against Iraq, citing the U.S. invasions of Panama and Grenada and the Israeli occupation of Palestinian land.

Japan's prime minister is forced to scrap the proposal to send troops to Saudi Arabia.

U.S. forces, now at 230,000, already include: four and a half U.S. Army divisions and other units with more than 120,000 troops and 1,000 tanks; one U.S. Marine expeditionary force and three expeditionary brigades with more than 45,000 troops; 3 U.S. aircraft carriers with 100 attack and fighter planes, the battleship *Wisconsin*, and 50 other warships; 500 air force and marine bombers, attack, and fighter planes.

Forces allied with Washington include **Syria:** 19,000 troops with 270 tanks in Saudi Arabia and 50,000 more troops on Syria's border with Iraq; **Turkey:** 95,000 troops on Turkey's border with Iraq; **Britain:** 15,000 troops, including the 7th Armoured Regiment with 120 tanks, along with 58 warplanes and 12 warships; **France:** 13,000 French troops, including an armored regiment, an infantry regiment, and a helicopter regiment, along with more than 75 planes and 14 warships, including the aircraft carrier *Clemenceau;* **Canada:** 1,700 troops, 3 warships, and 18 fighter planes; **Saudi Arabia:** 60,000 troops, with 180 planes and 8 ships, and a small force as part of the Gulf Cooperation Council's rapid deployment force; **Egypt:** 20,000 troops, with a second 7,000-man division and 400 tanks expected soon; **Kuwait:** 7,000 troops as part of the Gulf Cooperation Council's rapid deployment force; **Pakistan:** 5,000 troops; **Morocco:** at least 2,000 troops; **Bangladesh:** 2,000 troops; **Czechoslovakia:** 200 troops; **Argentina:** 100 troops; and **Senegal:** 500 troops. **Bahrain, Oman, Qatar,** and the **United Arab Emirates** have small numbers of troops deployed as part of the Gulf Cooperation Council's rapid deployment force, in addition to their regular armed forces.

Australia, Belgium, Denmark, Greece, Italy, the **Netherlands, Norway, Poland, Portugal,** the **Soviet Union,** and **Spain** have sent naval forces to the Gulf as part of the U.S.-led intervention.

Military units from thirty countries are now arrayed against Iraq. U.S. and allied forces face Iraqi regular troops estimated at 550,000, with 430,000 in or near Kuwait. Iraq has deployed 500 top-of-the-line T-72 tanks along with 1,000 T-62s and 4,000 older tanks. In addition, Iraq's reserves number 480,000.

November 8—Baker meets with Gorbachev and then Shevardnadze in Moscow. The Soviet leadership for the first time gives public support to possible military action as Shevardnadze says, "A situation may emerge that effectively could require" the use of force.

Japan's main opposition parties agree with the Japanese government on a new proposal to dispatch a civilian contingent including retired military officers to join U.S.-led forces in the Gulf. A Foreign Ministry official says, "We are pleased because even though the original proposal died, our work was not futile."

Bush, saying a massive new escalation is needed to provide "an adequate offensive military option," doubles the number of combat troops by ordering 200,000 more U.S. forces to the Gulf. More than 430,000 will be in the Gulf by early 1991. U.S. ground troops during the Vietnam War peaked at 543,000.

The new U.S. deployment includes more than three additional army divisions with more than 75,000 troops and 1,200 tanks—for a total of seven and a half divisions. The new units include the entire 1st and 3d Armored Divisions shifted from Germany and the entire 1st Infantry Division Mechanized from its U.S. base; the 2d Marine Expeditionary Force with 45,000 troops from Camp Lejeune and the 15,000-man 5th Marine Expeditionary Brigade from Camp Pendleton, both accompanied by armored units, which will bring the total Marine deployment to two-thirds of the entire Marine combat forces; and three Army National Guard armored brigades, which are to begin desert warfare training in the United States.

In the largest deployment of aircraft carriers since the Korean War, three more carriers and their battle groups will be dispatched, bringing the total now deployed to six of the fourteen carriers in the U.S. fleet. The battleship *Missouri* will join the battleship *Wisconsin* already in the region. An unspecified number of air force warplanes will be deployed in addition to the aircraft on the three new carriers.

The move puts more than 2,000 U.S. tanks in place and gives it superiority over Iraq in the most up-to-date tanks. With these redeployments, U.S. troop strength in Europe will be cut by 50 percent. U.S. officials expect to bring the 82d Airborne, a mobile rapid deployment force, back to the United States to be ready for other possible crises.

November 9—Cheney announces that U.S. forces will not be rotated until the Gulf crisis is over.

INDEX

PATHFINDER

Fidel Castro at the United Nations

Speaking to the General Assembly in 1979 as head of the Movement of Nonaligned Countries, Fidel Castro explained how the unjust economic system upheld by Washington is driving Third World countries to ruin, preparing explosive struggles. Calling for cancellation of the growing foreign debt Castro said, "We aspire to a new world order based on justice, on equity, and on peace." 46 pp., $2.50

Che Guevara at the United Nations

In December 1964 Ernesto Che Guevara addressed the UN General Assembly, representing Cuba. The U.S. government, Che said, is "the perpetrator of exploitation and oppression against the peoples of the world." His speech is included in *Che Guevara and the Cuban Revolution,* the major collection in English of Guevara's writings. 413 pp., $20.95

In Defense of Socialism

FIDEL CASTRO

In these speeches from 1988-89, Fidel Castro argues that the future belongs to socialism not capitalism. Castro also discusses Cuba's role in helping to defend the peoples of Angola and Namibia against the apartheid regime. 142 pp., $12.95

Che Guevara: Economics and Politics in the Transition to Socialism

CARLOS TABLADA

Examines Ernesto Che Guevara's contributions to building socialism. Guevara explains why the "dull instruments" of capitalist methods can only lead away from new social relations based on growing political consciousness and control by working people. 286 pp., $16.95